Competitive Strategies for Mid-Sized Law Firms

EDITED BY ALEX DAVIES

Commissioning editor
Alex Davies

Published by
Globe Law and Business Ltd
3 Mylor Close
Horsell
Woking
Surrey GU21 4DD
United Kingdom
Tel: +44 20 3745 4770
www.globelawandbusiness.com

ISBN: 978-1-78358-378-2
A catalogue record for this book is available from the British Library

Contents

Executive summary

Mid-sized law firms in today's legal marketplace are often given three choices: merge, grow, or die. That's accepted wisdom. Mid-sized firms may try to compete for profitable corporate litigation, deal, and other bread-and-butter work, but everyone knows they (1) don't have the IT and other systems heft to innovate with the big players, (2) don't have the scale to market and compete for global business, and (3) can't attract the talent they need to go head-to-head with Big Law on major work.

But what if that's wrong? What if mid-sized firms are in an ideal position to fix what's wrong with law practice today? *Competitive Strategies for Mid-Sized Law Firms* – a collection of essays by and about mid-sized firms – offers a new perspective.

Our opening chapter attempts to determine the parameters of what actually constitutes a mid-sized law firm, using both contemporary research, as well as the opinions of some of the book's contributors. Chapter two, by futurist John Alber, then debates the extent to which mid-sized law firms have the nimbleness and creativity to transform the legal services model in ways that clients are demanding. He argues that the revolution has already begun and that some visionary mid-sized firms and the companies that serve them are already taking the steps necessary to kick Big Law's can down the road and around the corner.

Continuing with this theme, it's been noted that the associate-heavy pyramid model characterizing Big Law has all the earmarks of a low quality model, ripe for innovation. In chapter three, Fred H Bartlit, partner at Bartlit Beck LLP, undertakes an analysis of why a smaller, partner-heavy business model is more conducive to producing high quality legal services than the current prevailing pyramid model – and how mid-sized firms are ideally placed to implement this structure.

Indeed, this may be the key to enabling mid-sized firms – and the law industry in general – fight off competition from other sectors. Much has been made over the past year about how the Big Four are preparing to take over the legal sector and how Big Law needs to respond. Equally, it has been stated that only Big Law has the deep pockets necessary to invest in the technology and innovation required to respond to this increased competition. However, not much has been said about how mid-sized law firms have a unique opportunity to successfully implement the changes necessary to out-compete their larger competitors. In chapter four, Stuart Wilson, former global chief marketing and business development officer, Dentons, and chief marketing officer at KPMG, believes there will be many winners and losers in the legal sector of the future, and among them will be many mid-sized law firms.

Chapter five continues with this perspective. Presenting views from BigLaw, mid-sized firms, and boutiques – and what she believes are the advantages and disadvantages of each – Nancey L Watson discusses how firms of various sizes and strengths can put themselves in the position to win more business and effectively compete in various markets by virtue of focusing on various levers of quality and/or service and delivery models.

In today's law firm environment, mid-sized law firms are in a unique position to compete. Some view this segment as one facing challenges in scale, footprint, and unable to afford the latest technological capabilities. Others see it as an agile, fleetfooted group able to provide tailored services with a strong personal touch, and one where firms can exploit mid-sized scale to be more responsive and tuned in to the clients they wish to serve, using new approaches to the practice. Chapter six, by Mark Medice, principal, LawVision LLC, takes the format of an interview with four mid-sized firms, discussing innovation, the competitive marketplace, managing change to transform practices, and data and technologies changing the practice for the next ten years.

The next two chapters are presented by companies working in close collaboration with mid-sized law firms, specifically in the field of technology. It is evident to any industry insider that there are more legal technology products now than there have ever been. From e-discovery to legal research to analytics to contract review, every niche and utility in legal is being addressed by legal tech companies. This explosion in available technology has created unprecedented opportunities for firms. It also poses a threat to those that choose to disregard this rise of innovation or merely acquire "shelfware," or technology that remains proverbially shrink-wrapped on a law firm shelf and not adopted years after purchase. As clients demand more value for less, certain mid-sized firms have leaned on technology to increase efficiency while maintaining accurate, high-caliber work product and minimizing risk, all while evening the playing field with the biggest firms. So how do you address these pressures without becoming disillusioned by the unending array of options and difficulties of technology adoption? To get a clearer picture, in chapter seven, Anand Upadhye, VP business development at Casetext, talks to some forward-thinking leaders at America's most prominent, innovative mid-sized and large law firms to learn from the best.

In chapter eight, Chris Austin, director of information governance, Bowman and Brooke, describes a mid-sized firm's subscription to an innovative product, including the challenges they faced purchasing and rolling the technology out and how they overcame those challenges. Chris provides actionable takeaways from a mid-sized firm that is modernizing in an industry that can be resistant to change.

Our final three chapters look at the culture of mid-sized law firms. Many firms will state their commitment to greater inclusivity and accessibility, but few will actually put in place schemes that command significant resources and input in order to guarantee it. Garden Court Chambers, a leading UK firm based in central London, is the exception. Its pioneering program "Access to the Bar for all" – which won Diversity Initiative of the Year at the 2017 UK Diversity Legal Awards – moves past the traditional one-week shadowing scheme format and aims to tackle the issues faced by young people from underprivileged backgrounds by providing long-term guidance and support in the form of extensive mentoring and funding. In chapter nine, Charlotte Ogilvie, marketing and communications executive, delves into the mechanics, context, and impact of the scheme, providing an inspiring and compelling example for other mid-sized firms to follow.

Chapter ten addresses the challenges associated with thinking and managing strategically in the current legal marketplace. Is the only strategy for mid-sized firms to merge and grow? Or, are there other ways to think strategically about market position and capture competitive advantages in ways that are largely independent of size? John Sterling, CMO at Sterne Kessler Goldstein & Fox, explores multiple dimensions of strategic thinking, including:

- The implications of scale in today's legal market – and how mid-size firms can approach competing with Big (even giant) Law;
- Options for creating strong defensive positions that are difficult (if not impossible) for competitors to overcome; and
- The logic of adopting so-called "indirect strategies" – effectively doing different things differently, creating sustained differentiation.

Compared to other professionals and the populace in general, lawyers score unusually high in several personality traits, including scepticism and autonomy, and low in others such as sociability and resiliency. These traits can be a real barrier to innovation – something that, as this book demonstrates, is a key issue mid-sized firms needs to address. Having reviewed the characteristics of successful innovation, chapter 11 posits that overcoming this barrier requires establishing a new frame of reference that encourages people to think, feel, and act differently. David Urbanik, chief operating officer at Halloran Sage, describes how one firm with a broad array of practice areas used a structured approach to define and build consensus around a common vision, purpose, values and brand promise. He details the specific processes that were used by teams to develop foundational tools, concluding by analysing the change in culture at the firm and how the foundational tools have enabled broader collaboration and innovation as well as leveraging the untapped leadership potential of not only the attorneys but all employees of the firm.

About the authors

John Alber serves as futurist for the Institute for Future of Law Practice and for the International Legal Technology Association. He writes, speaks, and consults widely, focusing on finding practical ways to reshape the delivery of legal services to suit a future demanding excellence far beyond substantive legal skills. Prior to his current role, John was a transportation industry CEO. Thereafter, he led Bryan Cave LLP to become one of the most innovative firms in the world, serving as its strategic innovation partner for more than 16 years. While at Bryan Cave, he also served for seven years on the firm's operating group (its management committee). John is an Emeritus fellow of the College of Law Practice Management. He has received a number of awards, both in the legal field and in information technology generally. Among other awards, he received ILTA's first ever Premiership Award, was named American Lawyer Media's first ever "Champion of Technology", was given a Lifetime Achievement Award by Law Technology News and recognized as one of the Top 25 CTOs in the world by Infoworld. In addition, while under his leadership, Bryan Cave received recognition as a *CIO Magazine* "Top 100 Company" and was twice recognized as ILTA's Most Innovative Firm.

Chris Austin is an established information management professional who focuses his work on transforming organizations with new processes and emerging technologies. With over 20 years of experience, Chris has overseen change in a variety of organizations including state and federal government, academia, publicly traded companies and law firms. His knowledge and experience include information systems, library services, and knowledge management. Recently, Chris has merged traditional library services with records functionality into a cohesive unit, breaking silos and transforming how data is consumed. Chris heads up the information governance efforts at Bowman and Brooke, including acquiring state of the art software, helping Bowman and Brooke continue its dominance as one of the premier product liability defense law firms.

Fred H Bartlit is a West Point graduate, winner of the competition for skill in the operation of the eight US Army Infantry Weapons, a US Army troop commander, a Distinguished Graduate of the US Army Ranger Detachment, and a US Army Ranger. As commander, he received the US Army Commendation Medal for "exceptional personal qualities, superior service, steadfast devotion to duty, vigorous personal leadership," and his command achieved best score of any such unit in the US Army for intercepting incoming targets with surface-to-air missiles.

He was first in his class in law school and has the top academic record in the 120-year history of the University of Illinois College of Law.

He is the subject of many books and publications, including *America's Top Trial Lawyers – Who They Are & Why They Win*. He has tried over 100 major cases in 24 states, the Virgin Islands and Scotland.

Mark Medice is a principal at LawVision and leads the financial performance and data science practice. He has over 20 years of leadership experience, providing and applying data solutions to the most pressing challenges facing law firm leaders. Mark spent over ten years at Thomson Reuters where he launched and led the peer monitor program. During that time, he created the Peer Monitor Index (PMI), which is widely used throughout the legal industry. Immediately prior to LawVision, Mark led new initiatives around analytics and metrics at Intapp. Law firm leaders rely on Mark's unparalleled experience in financial competitive intelligence and benchmarking, predictive analytics, industry performance, rates, pricing trends and strategy, profitability, and other critical issues facing firms today.

Charlotte Ogilvie is a communications professional with over five years' experience in the not-for-profit and private sector in the UK and internationally. She is a First Class History graduate from the School of Oriental and African Studies, and has worked across a broad range of communications, digital and editorial roles for the British Council in Bangkok, London, and Amman. Currently her focus is digital communications at Garden Court Chambers, a top-ranked barristers' set in central London that is committed to human rights, social justice, and equality.

John Sterling is chief marketing officer at Sterne Kessler Goldstein & Fox, a leading IP specialty firm based in Washington, DC. He is also the founding partner of Sterling Strategies, LLC. Prior to founding Sterling Strategies, John was a founding partner at Smock Sterling Strategic Management Consultants. He has over 30 years of experience in strategic management and market research. John has worked extensively with law and other professional service firms, as well as with industrial and consumer product companies and not-for-profit organisations. His work with TimeLine Theatre Company in Chicago won the Richard Goodman Strategic Planning Award for excellence in strategic planning from the Association for Strategic Planning. John is past president of the Strategic Management Association in Chicago and is a contributing editor to the business journal *Strategy & Leadership*.

Anand Upadhye is Casetext's vice president of business development. He presents Casetext's AI-backed legal research product to leading law firms, companies, and agencies. In that capacity, Anand works with CKOs, GCs, CIOs, senior partners, and library directors to determine the key pain points in their firms or companies. Additionally, he assists firms with messaging their technology acquisition to their attorneys and staff, as well as current and prospective clients. Before joining Casetext, Anand was an attorney for six years, first as a prosecutor and then as a litigator at a large firm. He presents internationally on legal technology, innovation, and rapid change in the legal industry at conferences, local bar associations, and law schools. He is the host of The Modern Lawyer podcast, where he interviews leaders in the legal industry. Anand attended the University of California, Berkeley and the University of San Diego.

David Urbanik began his business career as a strategic planning and mergers and acquisitions specialist for a large multi-national industrial corporation. In that role, he travelled the globe, providing advice and counsel to senior managers focused on developing and growing their businesses. He was deeply involved in a major corporate restructuring, managing the sale of 22 product lines and five major acquisitions. Working closely with some of the largest law firms in the world, Dave took the lead in negotiating the terms of a number of these transactions.

When his corporate employer became the victim of a hostile takeover, Dave found a new challenge in the then emerging field of the professional management of law firms. He was one of the early pioneers in formalizing and developing the role of financial analysis, marketing, planning, and information systems in the legal industry. Now, with more than 25 years of experience, he has served as a mentor and guide to many lawyers and non-lawyers alike in their personal professional development.

Dave has been cited as an innovator and has given presentations both locally and nationally on law firm management. He enjoys being surrounded by bright, creative people dedicated to furthering the best interests of their clients and takes pride in assisting in any way that he can.

Nancey L Watson, BEd. is president of NL Watson Consulting Inc. She has helped professional services firms win over $3 billion in competitive bids. Since 2012 she has worked almost exclusively with global, national, mid-size, and boutique law firms and in-house legal departments on RFPS and proposals.

She is an internationally recognized speaker who presents on topics such as pricing tactics, pricing master class, legal procurement's impact on law firm selection at in-house and law firm conferences including Thomson Reuters, Law Firm Marketing Partner Forum; Canadian Corporate Counsel Association National Conference and In-House Counsel World Summit; LawVision Group, Practice Partners Roundtable; and Legal Marketing Association, Eastern Canada Regional Conference.

Nancey is the author of ARK Group's *The Silver Bullet: How RFPS are won*, and creator of the workshop: *Strategic Proposal Management*. She is also the presenter of the accredited continuing professional development/continuing legal education course, *How Procurement Impacts Law Firm Selection*. As a contributing author for Thomson Reuters Legal Executive Institute she has articles published on procurement and law firm strategies and several podcasts on the Legal Executive Institute website. She can be reached at Nancey@NLWatsonConsulting.com.

Stuart Wilson is one of a few global marketing leaders with expertise as chief marketing officer of both Big Four and Big Law professional services firms. He is an innovative and transformational c-level marketing executive who leverages brand, business development, business intelligence, marketing communications, and digital marketing solutions to win, develop, and grow customers and clients. Throughout his career, he has advised many of the world's leading organizations regarding their marketing strategies and campaigns, including Coca-Cola, HSBC, InBev, P&G, American Express as well as Deloitte, PwC, EY and Latham & Watkins. He has deep experience working across six continents and numerous geographies, having lived and worked in London, Chicago, New York, and Toronto.

Chapter 1:

Does size matter? Defining the mid-sized law firm

By ARK Group

What defines a mid-sized firm? Is it headcount? Number of offices? The amount, and diversity, or practices? Or something less (perhaps more) tangible? According to research1 undertaken on optimum law firm size, there are five generally held "truisms" about the size of firms:

1. Capability – larger law firms are more capable of handling complex sophisticated legal matters than smaller firms;
2. Clients – larger law firms are more attractive to larger clients with more sophisticated legal issues than smaller firms;
3. Reputation – larger law firms have better reputations and name recognition than smaller firms;
4. Collegiality – larger law firms are less collegial than smaller firms; and
5. Profitability – larger law firms are more profitable than smaller firms.

Truisms, of course, can always be argued with, and there are a great many examples of law firms – large and small – that greatly contradict all of the above statements.

Ahead of the issues explored in this book, we asked some of its contributors to sum up what "mid-sized" meant to them – and why mid-sized firms are well-placed in today's market to succeed.

John Sterling, chief marketing officer, Sterne Kessler Goldstein & Fox:

Is a 500-attorney firm mid-sized? Sure, if your frame of reference is the AmLaw 50, then an AmLaw 200 firm is mid-sized. That is especially true if that firm aspires to being part of "Big Law". To generalize the point, defining what mid-sized is depends largely on what you are comparing it to (an elephant is mid-sized next to a brontosaurus). For most firms, "mid-sized" is best defined in the context of nearby (i.e. local and regional) competitors. In other words, mid-sized is a function of your size relative to other firms/offices in your primary (or only) city.

Chris Austin, director of records and information management, Bowman and Brooke:

Defining what it means to be a mid-sized law firm is more of an art than a science. A mid-sized law firm would be anything bigger than a solo practice but also anything smaller than a global firm.

More specifically, as a solo practitioner operating a law firm by yourself, you would lack the complexity that comes with operating as a team of other attorneys and legal professionals. That's not to say a solo practitioner does not have a name, reputation or brand to consider, but would lack the issues that consume mid-sized law firms.

Conversely, a law firm that is so large that the culture becomes too complex would also not meet the definition. If the culture of the firm feels more like a corporation instead of a law firm, then I do not think those firms would be considered mid-sized. This would include firms with large headcount, locations spread across the globe and broad practice areas.

What remains, is every other law firm, the middle.

Mark Medice, principal, LawVision LLC:

Mid-sized means a conscious decision to operate with a sense of service focus, flexibility, and intimacy. It provides freedom to be more agile but comes at potential risk of scale. Law firms today are required to decide who they are, and for those with a distinctive purpose well executed, their success remains unbound.

Fred H Bartlit, partner, Bartlit Beck LLP:

"Dunbar's number" is a suggested cognitive limit to the number of people with whom one can maintain stable social relationships – relationships in which an individual knows who each person is and how each person relates to every other person. This number was first proposed in the 1990s by British anthropologist Robin Dunbar, who found a correlation

between primate brain size and average social group size. By using the average human brain size and extrapolating from the results of primates, he proposed that humans can comfortably maintain 150 stable relationships. Dunbar explained it informally as "the number of people you would not feel embarrassed about joining uninvited for a drink if you happened to bump into them in a bar".

Proponents assert that numbers larger than this generally require more restrictive rules, laws, and enforced norms to maintain a stable, cohesive group. Dunbar theorized that "this limit is a direct function of relative neocortex size, and that this in turn limits group size [...] the limit imposed by neocortical processing capacity is simply on the number of individuals with whom a stable inter-personal relationship can be maintained".

The reason for going with the rough Dunbar number is that law is a business where the assets are people and the work is all done by people. Quality in a people business like law is NOT scalable. Hiring 200 associates a year is a recipe for watering down firm personnel quality.

A leader cannot choose people, mentor them, train them when he does not know them, it is just that simple. When I was a troop commander, my unit was about 160 men or so. I knew all of them, including background, where they came from, their strengths, interests, and so on. I was decorated for having one of best units in the US Army and I could not have done this with 2,000 men. A law firm leader cannot build grow, lead, and mentor a group which is too large for him to know really well. It is just that simple.

David Urbanik, chief operating officer, Halloran Sage:

I tend to categorize law firms as small, mid, and large based on the complexity of the business organization and the structure required to manage it.

Small firms tend to have a single layer of non-attorney management, typically in the form of a firm administrator who handles accounting, billing, human resources, etc. and a managing partner or partners who are full-time practicing attorneys. Generally this structure can effectively handle up to about 50 attorneys.

Unless the firm has a very focus practice and a single location, once you get much above 50 attorneys, you generally need a two-layer non-lawyer management structure comprised of an executive director or COO with several direct reports who manage individual administrative functions (accounting, human resources, marketing, IT, etc.) to operate efficiently. In these firms, the managing partner in the vast majority of cases is still a practicing attorney but will likely be devoting 25-50 percent of her or his time to firm management. I would consider these to be mid-sized firms.

At some point as firms grow, the complexity of the business requires a third level of non-lawyer management. This may occur either in the form of subsections of specific departments (for example, a director of business development, a director of special events and a director of communications all reporting to a chief marketing officer) or as administrative management teams dedicated to specific practice groups. In these firms, the managing partner has a greatly reduced practice or is not actively practicing at all. I would consider a firm with these characteristics to be a large firm. I think it would be very unusual for a firm of much less than 150 attorneys to require this type of structure. At the same time, once you start approaching 250+ attorneys, it probably becomes very difficult to manage without it.

Ultimately, the break-over from small to mid-sized to large firm will depend on a number of factors – diversity of practice, number of offices, sophistication of the work done by the firm, etc. However, based on the foregoing theory of complexity of business organization, I would think the vast majority of mid-sized firms will have between 50 and 250 attorneys.

Nancey Watson, president of NL Watson Consulting Inc.:

The classification of a mid-sized firm means different things to different people. Some characterize the Am 200 as being mid-sized while other localities would consider the headcount of a mid-sized Am 200 firm as being a big firm. By mere headcount it is difficult to give one definition as to what mid-sized means. Typically, they are not international or global in scope. I think, as a rule, they encompass more than a handful of lawyers and reflect a certain culture – less bureaucratic, more connected with their lawyers, and prominent enough to be recognized in their locality. I also look at them as being full service or providing a number of services.

Stuart Wilson, former global chief marketing and business development officer, Dentons, and chief marketing officer at KPMG:

> *How does one define mid-law? I think any traditional definition of the legal market at this time is a challenge, and as such nearly all market definitions need to be reviewed and potentially re-evaluated. For example, should Big Law, which is often defined by revenue and number of lawyers, include PwC, which has more fee-earning lawyers than any another law firm? Does the fact that many of the world's largest law firms continue to grow through acquisition, not move the threshold of how one should define mid-law? Should mid-law, recently defined by the Legal Executive Institute as firms outside the Am Law 200 to firms with 35 lawyers, also include some alternate legal service providers? Ultimately, I believe that the future definition of law firms will be as much driven by how they adopt technology, refine their management systems, and define their client service approach, as by their size. In the future, size may have little correlation to success. Instead, firms that adapt and harness new ways of thinking will be the firms of the future.*

Reference

1. https://www.edge.ai/category/edge-international-review/

Chapter 2:
Start the revolution in the middle

By John Alber, futurist, International Legal Technology Association & Institute for the Future of Law Practice

"Listen," consultants are always telling mid-sized law firms, "You've got three choices in today's legal marketplace: merge, grow, or die."

And that's accepted wisdom. Law practice economics don't lie. Mid-sized firms may try to compete for profitable corporate litigation, deal, and other bread-and-butter work. But, everyone knows they (1) don't have the IT and other systems heft to innovate with the big players, (2) don't have the scale to market and compete for global business, and (3) can't attract the talent they need to go head-to-head with Big Law on major work.

But what if that's wrong? What if mid-sized firms are in an ideal position to fix what's wrong with law practice today? Could it be that the revolution has already begun and some visionary mid-sized firms and the companies that serve them are already taking the steps necessary to kick Big Law's can down the road and around the corner? Might they have exactly the nimbleness and creativity to transform the legal services model in ways that clients are demanding? And can we hope that creativity perfuses the whole model and fixes what desperately needs fixing?

Well, we'll see. But first, let's talk about what's broken.

How unhappy can you make us?

Clients have been telling Big Law for years that their service model is abysmal. Association of Corporate Counsel (ACC) surveys[1] highlight year after year that lawyers don't return phone calls, that they are difficult to reach, and unresponsive. Altman Weil, BTI Consulting, and others capture the repeated complaint that lawyers don't trouble themselves to learn their clients' businesses. And, as though that weren't bad enough, only a small fraction of chief legal officers surveyed by the ACC believe firms are willing to change their service models. Big Law just keeps on keeping on.

These conditions have led to an unprecedented level of activism by law departments. The rise of legal operations functions, the introduction of procurement disciplines into the acquisition of legal services, the formation of groups such as the Corporate Legal Operations Consortium (CLOC), the creation of the ACC Value Challenge, extraordinary push-back on pricing and staffing decisions –all are dramatic responses to these perceived shortcomings.

So what are Big Law firms doing in response to all this very vocal complaining? Well, they're doing what they do best – raising prices.

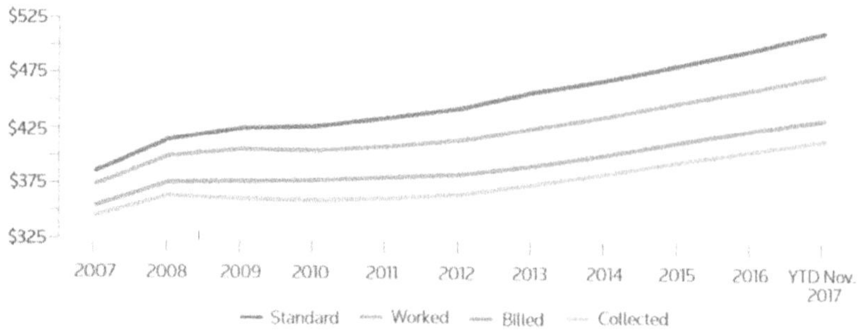

Figure 1: Rate progression.

Source: Thomson Reuters Peer Monitor.

Defining the opportunity

Altman Weil's 2016 survey[2] captured the essence of the opportunity that inheres – for someone – in these law department complaints:

> *"Among the reasons that law departments switch law firms, the themes of problematic service, cost and efficiency appear prominently. In the last 12 months, 53 percent of law departments say they shifted a portfolio of work worth $50,000 or more because of a client service issue; 41 percent switched to another firm in pursuit of lower fees; and 30 percent moved their work to a firm that was more effective in managing matters.*

> *"Every year since 2009, the survey has asked law departments to assess law firms' seriousness about changing their legal service delivery model. In 2016, for the eighth year running, CLOs rated law firms at a median three on a zero to ten scale in which zero equals 'not at all serious' about change and ten equals 'doing everything they can.'"*

The 2017 Georgetown Report, from the Center for the Study of the Legal Profession at Georgetown University Law Center and Thomson Reuters Legal Executive Institute,[3] goes further:

> *"Driven by strong internal pressures to reduce the overall cost of legal services, clients over the past decade have been increasingly willing to embrace a broad range of strategies to enhance the value they receive for their 'legal spend'. A linchpin of these strategies has been a growing willingness on the part of clients to disaggregate or unbundle the services they seek from particular outside providers, and this, in turn, has led to a steady erosion of the traditional law firm franchise."*

These market conditions would be opportunity enough for entrepreneurial firms of any size. But the opportunity for mid-sized firms is amplified by the astounding passivity of Big Law firms in recognizing and responding to client complaints. Yes, Big Law firms talk about changes in the market. And sometimes they appoint chief innovation officers or the like to "think" about change. But do they change?

Not enough for clients. That inaction has created a growth industry that has come to be called "New Law". Services such as Rocket Lawyer[4] and LegalZoom[5] are turning automated document assembly and online decision trees into an entirely new infrastructure for the delivery of legal services. And, while those companies started out in the consumer sphere, they are now encroaching on valuable start-ups, as well as small and mid-sized business markets.

Legal Process Outsourcers (LPOs) have transformed the economics of eDiscovery, and cut, especially, Big Law out of very profitable revenue streams. Virtual entities such as Axiom,[6] Counsel on Call,[7] and VLP[8] are reformulating what it means to be a firm. Blockchain-based companies are actively developing smart contract solutions in the financial and consumer goods sectors that cut lawyers out of the equation. Alternate dispute resolution services are springing up to remedy the cost, delay, and unfairness inherent in an overloaded court system. And all of this is clearly just a beginning. Watson[9] is waiting in the wings and clients are lined up waiting to use AI to further erode Big Law's hold on premium legal services.

The mid-sized opening

Which brings us to mid-sized firms. It turns out that the major mid-market constraints that have, over the years, prompted consultants to recommend merging or accelerated growth may no longer apply.

Take the assumption that only large firms can capitalize and manage the technology platforms necessary to compete for sophisticated legal work. The rise of SaaS (Software as a Service) and cloud-based solutions now puts powerful technologies within reach of mid-sized budgets. And vendors such as LogicForce Consulting[10] are available to spread the cost of technology management across many mid-sized firms. So, those firms can now compete head-to-head with Big Law in areas such as auditable cybersecurity (especially important to financial institutions), state-of-the-art eDiscovery, and mobile practice solutions. Technology, in other words, is no longer a barrier.

What about other advantages of scale that accrue to Big Law? Can mid-sized firms offset those too? Yes, absolutely. Law firm networks such as Lex Mundi,[11] TerraLex,[12] Meritas,[13] and InterLaw[14] have been working since the late 1980s to extend the reach of mid-sized firms through global branding, expertise sharing, and other cooperative efforts. And these networks are becoming quite sophisticated. At some point, clients have to wonder how much difference truly exists between a well-run network and a Big Law firm Swiss verein in terms of branding, global reach, and sophistication. One looks pretty much like the other.

Once problems of technology and scale are solved, client satisfaction becomes a matter of available expertise and reforming Big Law's ponderous service model. The real competition –between New Law, Old Law, Big Law, and anyone else who wants to weigh in now –will be over redesign of the service model.

Back in the 1980s, the big firms could still make the case that armies of superbly educated, fabulously expensive associates were necessary to sift through discovery documents in litigation. How else, the firms argued, could you expect to find the one smoking gun in the midst of a warehouse of documents?

How indeed? Try automation, efficient work processes, trained specialists rather than untrained generalists… and so on. The case has already been made that Big Law armies are not necessarily any advantage.

eDiscovery automation and LPO specialization broke the back of the associate leverage argument in eDiscovery, and began to undermine associate leverage across all practice areas. Billing guidelines propagated by many large clients now prohibit billing for first years, sometimes second years, and force the cost of coming up the learning curve from clients back to firms.

All of this creates a huge opening for firms that are willing to re-examine their assumptions and alter them to meet the demand for real innovation and service.

Perhaps the foremost example of a mid-sized firm that meets head-on the sorts of client demands discussed above is Bartlit Beck.[15] That firm is not a new creation. Fred Bartlit left Kirkland & Ellis to form the firm more than 20 years ago. But the market conditions he described[16] that gave the firm its opening are just as prevalent today as when Bartlit Beck started.

The working assumption of the large firm was that the more hours a project took, and the more lawyers involved, the better the end quality. This assumption in turn drove a business model that seemed, to us, even more peculiar, resulting in:

- Experience becoming devalued. Associate turnover was fostered. Most associates were terminated as they gained experience. It was typical of large firms to hire classes of 150 each year, and terminate most of them by the eighth year. The result was that the lion's share of a large firm's workforce was kept intentionally inexperienced;
- The legal process being very susceptible to use of time-saving technology. Yet most associates, and almost no partners in charge, were able to use technology; and
- The hour-based fee model in inefficient firms being more profitable than a relatively more efficient firm.

Bartlit Beck addressed those problems of the Big Law model by:

- Eliminating hourly billing;
- Working only on a fixed fee basis, with a results bonus;
- Shifting from high associate leverage to high partner leverage;
- Creating a true apprenticeship for the associates the firm does hire;
- Using their low associate leverage and apprenticeship models to attract the best law school and law clerk talent;
- Avoiding all lateral hiring; and
- Leveraging all the best technology, not because it is innovative, but because efficiency is now a benefit rather than a detriment to the revenue model.

The result of this client-focused service model has been steady growth for Bartlit Beck, a reputation for expertise and outcomes that rivals or exceeds that of most Big Law litigation practices, and a client list any Big Law litigation department would be proud of.

While Bartlit Beck is not a full service firm and mid-sized firms trying to emulate Big Law's smorgasbord approach to practice may not see the fit, its policies very precisely address the complaints that most clients are now voicing about Big Law. The template has been cut, the exemplar proven.

If the Bartlit Beck example is so good, why haven't more mid-sized firms taken such "radical" steps to meet client demand? In part, the "grow, merge or die" advice propagated by consultants has taken its toll. "Bartlit Beckizing" your firm isn't on the menu.

But it needs to be. Because our clients need legal services designed for humans, not for law firms. And if law firms don't meet the demand, then New Law and other latter day creations will grow to fill the void.

References

1. www.acc.com/resource-library/client-satisfaction-survey
2. www.altmanweil.com/dir_docs/resource/e32f33b3-eeb3-4af6-82c8-4f6f7d9824f6_document.pdf
3. https://static.legalsolutions.thomsonreuters.com/static/pdf/peer-monitor/S042201-Final.pdf
4. www.rocketlawyer.co.uk/
5. www.legalzoom.com/uk/
6. www.axiomlaw.com/
7. https://counseloncall.com/who-we-are/
8. www.vlplawgroup.com/
9. www.ibm.com/watson
10. www.logicforce.com/
11. www.lexmundi.com/
12. www.terralex.org/
13. www.meritas.org/
14. www.interlaw.com/
15. www.bartlit-beck.com/
16. 16www.abajournal.com/legalrebels/article/the_competitive_analysis_underlying_bartlit_beck/

Chapter 3: Turning the prevailing law firm business model upside down

By Fred Bartlit, partner, Bartlit Beck LLP

The US market for legal services is huge, currently estimated at over $400 billion annually. Law firms are led by some of the most intelligent, ambitious people in the world. One would expect this to be a quality-driven market. Yet law firms have universally pursued a business structure that is antithetical to producing quality legal services.

Today's prevailing large law firm structure is of course a pyramid, which is light on experienced partners and heavy on inexperienced associates. Typically, we see the structure as illustrated in Figure 1.

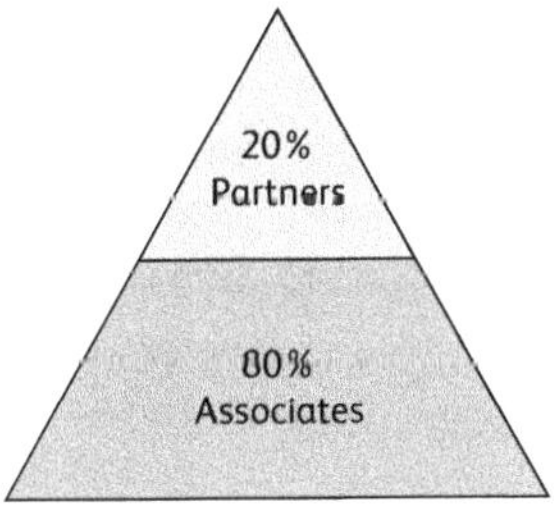

Figure 1: The typical law firm "pyramid" structure.

Now, it is pretty much assumed throughout the law business that the pyramid structure of Big Law firms represents the pinnacle of quality in the delivery of legal services. Yet, we will see that the pyramid is, in reality, incompatible with quality in legal services. In fact, we will see that if we started with a clean sheet to design a structure focusing on quality we would turn the entire existing pyramid *upside down*, thereby *reversing* almost every law firm function.

In this process, we will learn that the current pyramid model is, according to the analysis of Peter Drucker in his seminal 1984 book *Innovation and Entrepreneurship*, a classic example of an industry structure that is ripe for dramatic innovation.

Let's start by examining the thinking behind the prevailing assumption that the pyramid model adopted by all Big Law firms results in the highest quality legal services.

The law business today is very high stakes and considered extremely complicated, requiring both intensive legal analysis, and marshalling, organizing, and presenting massive and complex factual material. It is thought that this process requires large numbers of associates, each assigned to different aspects of the project and analyzing all parts of each aspect down to a molecular level. And, because few associates have ever seen a trial, most of this critical, difficult work is done by associates with no experience in what they are doing.

This thinking leads to the assumption that very large law firms organized into the associate-heavy pyramid are the only way to effectively handle such projects.

Now, why do we say that this pyramid model has for a long time existed as a classic example of a weird, anomalous business model ripe for innovation and change? To explain this, we turn to Peter Drucker.

Drucker tells us that the most likely target for innovation is a business model where there are big "discrepancies" between what it is generally *assumed* that the model achieves and how the model *actually* operates. The law firm pyramid fits Drucker's analysis to a T – it is *assumed* by law firms and most clients that the associate-heavy pyramid structure best leads to high quality legal services. Yet, we will see that this assumption is flat wrong, so that Drucker would conclude the pyramid has, for decades, cried out for major innovation and change. This is because the pyramid does not lead to high quality legal services as is assumed. In reality, it leads to an opposite result.

You get what you pay for

In the associate-heavy pyramid model, firm profits are based on hours expended. Clients pay for hours expended. The more hours the law firm expends, the more the client pays. Of course, when firm profits are based on hours expended, that is what clients will get: *hours*. As the old saying goes: "*You get what you pay for*".

The core pyramid principle that "the more hours expended, the better for the law firm" leads to a series of weird market anomalies, all of which are inconsistent with high quality:

- Basing profits on hours expended on a project rewards inefficiency. An inexperienced worker generates more dollars of revenue than an experienced, skilled worker;

- Experience is very important in dealing with complex legal issues. Experience is especially important in trial work. Former Federal Judge Prentice Marshall observed: "a trial lawyer does not know what to do in a jury trial until he has had the equivalent of 20 jury trials". Yet in the associate-heavy model, most of the time expended is put in by inexperienced associates who have never seen a trial;
- A profit formula based on huge amounts of hours put in by raw rookies who have never done it before is not a recipe for high quality in complex projects;
- The normal business incentives to invest in training and project efficiencies are pretty much non-existent. Disincentives for efficiencies is not a recipe for high quality;
- To the contrary, associates' compensation is most often based on "hours expended" rather than efficiencies and results. When workers are paid bonuses for "extra" hours, the client is assured of getting "extra hours". Again, not a recipe for high quality;
- There are no industry metrics for quality. There are no databases providing guidance on how many hours and how much money particular kinds of projects should require. Instead, it is simply *assumed* by all parties that the more associates on a matter and the longer they take to do their work, the higher the quality. This is most assuredly not a recipe for high quality;
- Focus on results is blunted. Law firms profits do not depend solely on results but, in large part, on numbers of associates on a matter, the amount of hours it takes them to do the work, and how long the matter takes to get resolved. Years of such costly, massive efforts ending in a settlement are pretty much just as profitable (or even more profitable) for a firm as securing a great result in a relatively short time. This is NOT a recipe for high quality.
- The normal business incentives to mentor and train young professionals are attenuated. Young professionals become less valuable as they gain experience, become more efficient, and take fewer hours to accomplish projects. Additionally, as their pay increases, the margins per hour are likely reduced. The result is that a very high percentage of associates are terminated after five to eight years, after they have become experienced and, at last, know what they are doing;

- The associate-heavy model creates an inefficient "bottom up" workflow in which experienced guidance on a project is often delayed until after untold hours have been wasted by layers of inexperienced associates. A project first planned by an associate who has never seen a trial is then funneled through layers of more senior associates and junior partners, increasing both cost and complexity by orders of magnitude;
- The profitability of multitudes of associates has driven an avalanche of mergers, even though "quality" in human capital is not scalable. Law firm mergers inevitably result in lower overall law firm quality in the newly merged firm;
- The "hours trump all" mania and resulting large size results in poor family life, narrow personalities, and loss of agility and innovation; and
- Thus, there is almost NO real innovation in law. Industry conferences routinely do not focus on "improving quality" as a desirable innovation, much less on how to change the model to achieve it. Instead, ways and means of increasing rates, incentivizing associates to work more hours, and assuring all billed hours are collected are emphasized. Lately we have seen more and more topics like "Becoming a skilled timekeeper" on conference agendas.

We thus see clearly that the associate-heavy pyramid model has many major discrepancies between what the market assumes the model achieves and its reality. Peter Drucker would salivate over a business model that his analysis proves is a big, fat target ripe for an innovation that would drive a move from "hours billed" to "higher quality".

Now we turn to the question of how a normally intelligent person would attack such a "big, fat, ripe innovation target". If any of us were starting with a clean sheet of paper, and told to come up with a new law firm structure, focusing on a dramatic improvement to quality, what would be our first thoughts?

Of course, trying to improve the current pyramid model is not the way to begin. That would boil down to "doing the same old wrong things better". Instead, we must identify the major problems that need solving and figure out what structure will eliminate these problems.

The major problems are:

- Most of the work being done by relative rookies who have never done it before; and

- Profit is not heavily driven by results but by how long it takes bring the matter to an end.

Accordingly, a logical first step is imagining a law firm structure that addresses these two problems and thereby also eliminates the horde of weird market anomalies resulting from the current pyramid.

Here's an idea: since the current model is so screwed up, and we know it will only get worse if we tinker with it at the margins, why not just toss out the current model and forget about it? Why not make the biggest, most dramatic change/innovation imaginable and simply turn the old wrong law firm structure upside down?

Turning the model upside down

I wonder what it would look like if we turned the current model upside down and how it would it eliminate all the problems set forth above? Let's take a look in Figure 2.

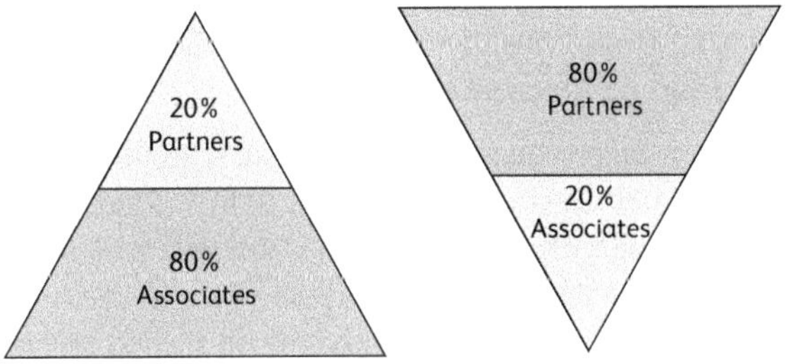

Figure 2: The current pyramid model, and the pyramid turned upside down.

Hmmm. What does this dramatic move accomplish? A new law firm structure that is *partner-heavy*. This means most of the work is now done by a cadre of highly skilled, very experienced and efficient partners, and a very few, carefully selected associates in training, as members of small teams working with and mentored by the cadre of experienced trial lawyers.

The new model is more like SEAL Team Six or the US Army Ranger Detachment than it is like Sears, Roebuck or the Russian Duma – fast moving, flexible, innovative, motivated to train new recruits to the hilt, and led by dedicated, motivated professionals.

It is immediately apparent that in the upside down model, most of the work will be done or supervised from day one by experienced, highly skilled trial lawyers. This, alone, is a giant step to higher quality, compared to the traditional pyramid with its focus on most of the work being done by associates who have never done it before.

But this giant structural difference is only the beginning. Once this change is made, it is easy to think of other policies that could then be implemented, driving the new model to much higher quality.

Additional quality support policies include:

- Instead of mass hirings of as many as 200 associates per year, hire only one to two very high potential associates for intense training programs;
- *All associates are permanent.* No "up or out". The result is a powerful incentive to train and mentor them, and guarantee the most experienced cadre of expert trial lawyers in the world;
- Because the new model will drive better results achieved with much greater efficiency, a radical new method of charging clients for the services of this cadre of experts will be required. Hourly billing will be replaced by charging clients based on the results achieved rather than how long the matter takes and how many associates can be assigned to the matter;
- The quality-driven firm will try a much higher percentage of its cases compared to the hours-driven firms. Small teams and many trials will mean that almost every lawyer will have a trial role every year. This will mean that the lawyers in the quality firm will steadily become more experienced, more skilled lawyers, while the hours firms will steadily fall behind in experience and skill;
- Associates will have trial roles and will be personally prepared and drilled for these roles by skilled, experienced members of the trial lawyer cadre, which will dramatically accelerate the development of associates into expert trial lawyers;
- Because all lawyers are permanent, training and mentoring will become paramount, and quality firms will institute internal "universities" with firm partners and outside resources regularly teaching trial and technology skills;
- Workflow on projects will be led from the top down instead of the current "bottom up" in which first drafts of all work are done by those who have no experience in actual trials. Experienced trial lawyers will lay out projects and circulate to both clients and other team members for ideas, corrections, and additions. This will both increase quality and cut inefficiencies;

- The new quality law firm will discourage "face time", ending the demeaning culture of celebrating those who work evenings and weekends in the office; and
- The new quality firm will also insist on true collegiality with everyone in it together, replacing the "shark infested waters" of many hourly firms.

The new upside down model and the above supporting policies will thus create an entirely different, far superior work–life experience for both clients and lawyers. Most importantly, the resulting far superior quality will drive trial success rates to the 80 percent range.

Lawyers will be rewarded for fast, efficient, high quality work rather than being "winners" in a mind-numbing culture of "hours". All lawyers will have normal, happy lives, able to spend time with their spouses and children, producing far better trial lawyers, compared to the current hourly wage slaves.

The resulting culture of true collegiality with everyone pitching in to help each other will produce still another major step forward in the new "quality" law firm, as well as making the new firm a wonderful place to live your professional life.

Perhaps the most significant of all the myriad of quality driving advantages of the new firm is the impact of the new firm and new culture on recruiting.

The most high potential law school graduates will ALL desire, most of all, to work in the new quality firm. The lifestyle, training, mentoring, personal collegial relationships, and professional rewards will drive the very top prospects to the new firm, thus adding an order of magnitude to the enhanced quality of the firm.

Why in the world have NO firms figured out the benefits of the quality model and adopted it? Wouldn't anyone reading this be convinced and long for the world and life of the quality firm? Wouldn't they have a dawning realization that the current pyramid model is upside down and backwards? That no top "star" in any area of professional endeavor would want to work by the hour? That Michael Jordan would never have played basketball being paid by the hour? That it is common sense to reward what is actually accomplished, not how long and slow it took to do it? That the current model is dehumanizing and destructive of both professional and personal life?

Isn't it crystal clear that the partner-heavy model is clearly far superior with regard to quality of legal services, and every other possible standard. That the new quality model is a textbook example of Peter

Drucker's explanation of the most valuable innovation as "a new business model that exploits obvious market anomalies in an important field of commerce".

One would expect that the extremely intelligent and ambitious leaders of law firms would have long ago seen the benefits of business model innovation and adopted the upside down quality model. Yet, it appears that NO Big Law firm has ever done this. For years at my lectures, I have asked the audience "Do any of you know any major law firm that tries billion dollar cases for Fortune 50 companies that focuses purely on the quality model and cannot be hired by the hour?" The answer is always "no". (Of course, large firms today often advertise that they offer "alternative fee deals". But there is no change in the pyramid structure and such fee deals are by far the exception rather than the rule.)

Applying the model to mid-sized firms

The new upside down high quality model is perfectly suited to the mid-sized firms that are the subject of this book. Mid-sized firms are inherently much more agile and flexible than large firms. They are generally led by a smaller group of strong leaders able to make important decisions without the endless deliberations characterizing committee-ridden large firms. I once worked in a large firm that actually had a "Committee of Committees" like the US Congress. You can imagine the deliberations over any significant issue.

Changing from an associate-heavy firm to a partner-heavy firm is simply not possible when a decision with massive financial consequences and personnel impact must be filtered through a complex committee system.

Second, the quality model only works in a firm where it is the only model. I know from experience that it is not possible to have both the associate-heavy hourly model and the partner-heavy quality model in the same firm. The existence, side by side, of the two models makes it impossible to point out the myriad fatal flaws of the pyramid.

Third, the high quality inherent in the partner-heavy model is a clear distinguishing factor vs Big Law competitors. It is easy to explain and establish the "quality" difference in the marketplace.

Finally, the quality model is much more attractive to the top high potential law students in the US. The small teams, mentoring, training and potential to have a family life that are not possible in an hourly pyramid firm attracts the very top recruits and thus enables the mid-sized firm to easily out-recruit the large firms.

Of course, the proposed new model is not hypothetical. In chapter two, John Alber points out that the partner-heavy model is a proven model that works amazingly well in a mid-sized law firm. I know he is right because I have lived the partner-heavy model for 26 years. Bartlit Beck – perhaps the only true upside down pyramid firm in the US – has been able to consistently achieve outstanding success in the recruiting wars with Big Law. As a result, 68 percent of the lawyers in that firm are former US District Court or Federal Courts of Appeals clerks. And, in the last 15 years, 25 percent of its new recruits have been US Supreme Court clerks.

Why not Big Law?

So, how do we explain the fact that no Big Law firm has adopted the new quality model? Maybe it is because of another of Peter Drucker's theories of what makes a great innovation: A *market innovation that is difficult or impossible for competitors to match.*

The upside down quality model meets this test perfectly. Lawyers, by their nature, are averse and resistant to change. And, it is likely impossible, as a practical matter, to change a 1,500 lawyer firm from 20 percent partners to 80 percent partners – certainly not quickly.

So, instead of innovating to change a clearly inferior law firm structure model, Big Law just keeps trying to do the same old wrong things better: "get the hours up", "get the rates up", and "improve collections".

Likely another reason why the quality innovation is difficult or impossible for competitors to match is the science of paradigm shifts. Social scientists who study the science of resistance to change have concluded, over and over for decades, that "*the last persons to see the advantages of an innovation are those who have been most successful in the old, outmoded paradigms*".

The leaders of law firms have done very well financially with the pyramid model. Paradigm shift science would mean that it is not that they disagree with a quality innovation. It would mean that they simply cannot see the advantages of a new model because they have done so well personally financially in the old "hours" pyramid model.

Perhaps our efforts in these pages to compare the old model and the quality model may get some of these leaders to thinking, hence the reason I wrote this piece.

Chapter 4:
Big Four, Big Law, Mid Law – how mid-sized firms can beat their competitors

By Stuart Wilson, former global chief marketing and business development officer, Dentons

Much has been made over the past year about how the Big Four are preparing to take over the legal sector and how Big Law needs to respond. Equally, much has been stated that it is only Big Law that has the deep pockets necessary to invest in the technology and innovation required to respond to this increased competition. However, not as much has been said about how mid-sized law firms have a unique opportunity to successfully implement the changes necessary to out-compete their larger competitors.

While it is unquestionable that the legal sector is undergoing dramatic change, from innovations in legal process management, to AI, to large-scale client data management, to a new focus on client service, few law firms, big or small, are clear on how to harness these changes for future success. In reality there will be many winners and losers in the legal sector of the future. Amongst the winners will be many mid-sized law firms. Most notably those who can blend the best of what differentiates them, while empowering their leaders and harnessing their lower cost structures.

A small list of the necessary actions includes:

- Shaping and implementing a clear vision and strategy, which while seemingly obvious, is remarkably hard for many firms;
- Ensuring partner collaboration is core to firm culture, including taking active steps to ensure collaboration is valued in actions as well as words;
- Empowering managing partners to act, by ensuring they have the necessary structure and support to lead the firm;
- Investing in technology in a manner that values the successful operation of technology, as much as the original capital investment; and

- Consistently putting clients first. Another seemingly obvious action that eludes so many law firms.

While many of these actions seem obvious, few firms, large or small, are able to achieve their successful implementation. What's nice about this potential path to success for mid-sized law firms is that it requires limited capital investment, large-scale innovation, complex technology adoption, or radical change. In reality it needs what most mid-sized law firms have – a strong community of partners that can shape a clear vision, a willingness to support leadership through change, and an unwavering focus on clients.

Why change?

For many law firms the foundational question of "why change?" has yet to be answered. While there is much coverage in industry media about how the legal sector is undergoing a radical transition, many law firm partners see this change as distant, maybe even irrelevant.

For example, a 2018 study of the legal industry by Altman Weil,[1] which included data from more than 400 US law firms, noted that 59 percent of respondent law firms said their partners were not feeling enough economic pain to drive material change. Interestingly, these same firms recognized that many of their partners were not operating at pre-financial crisis level billable hours, and that close to 60 percent of all firms surveyed were seeing significant declines in profitability due to this over capacity.

Much of this unwillingness to embrace change has been laid at the feet of "lawyers coasting to retirement", with 40 percent of firms stating this was a major issue. While there is no question that the ageing partner demographic is making the transition to a new way of thinking more difficult, to place the blame on this group is simplistic.

What is driving this change?

There are a number of major transitions occurring that are driving the need to change. Here are some of the substantive ones.

Clients as drivers of change

Throughout history, as innovations emerge, economies change, and industries adapt, one finds that it is often customers and outsiders that drive the change. Basic liberal market economics necessitates that businesses seek more efficient ways of delivering their products and services. Outsiders – those not hamstrung by legacy thinking – create innovations that respond to customer demand. Within the industry there are those companies/firms that recognize the change and drive internal change to respond to the new market dynamics. This is both the challenge and opportunity for mid-sized law firms.

In many ways the changes that impact law firms have been decades in their development. One of the more substantive drivers is new procurement models being brought to the legal sector. In reality the legal sector is just the last in a line of professional services that have been put through the wringer by procurement teams. Corporations large and small are using ever more sophisticated approaches to managing their professional services costs – whether it be RFPs, AFAs (Alternative Fee Arrangements), reverse auctions, or competitive pricing and service benchmarking.

Many of these companies are taking experiences learned by procuring ever cheaper widgets and applying the lessons to professional services. Ask any advertising executive, Big Four audit partner, or professional engineer, and they will regale one with the horror stories of what procurement has done to their profitability. For lawyers, many of whom still think they are different from these other professional services, the same systems are being applied, much to their chagrin.

Technology will never replace lawyers

As Bill Gates has been quoted,[2] "We always overestimate the change that will occur in the next two years and underestimate the change that will occur in the next ten. Don't let yourself be lulled into inaction."

According to *In-House Counsel's 2018 Legal Tech Buyers Guide*[3] there has been a more than 65 percent increase in legal tech companies using AI over the prior 12-month period, creating more than 67 AI-based legal tech companies. Additionally, the guide highlighted the fact that for the second year in a row, just under a quarter of a billion dollars was invested in legal technology start-ups. With these figures it doesn't take much to realize that legal technology is here to stay.

But it's not just about the competition. Clients are at the core of this drive toward harnessing technology. A recent survey by CLOC (Corporate Legal Operations Consortium),[4] whose stated mission is "to help legal operations professionals and other core corporate legal industry players optimize the legal service delivery models" sought the views of 213 companies spending more that $6.3 billion in legal services. The survey found that these companies were embracing technology at an unprecedented rate. Of the survey participants, 78 percent had harnessed e-billing systems to manage their law firm invoices, 46 percent had implemented dashboard systems to evaluate the performance of their law firms, and 29 percent were using technology to manage their workflow.

Everywhere one looks, technology is driving change in the delivery of legal services and this will not miss mid-sized law firms.

Big Four knocking at the door

The entry of the Big Four accounting firms into the legal sector is being seen as shifting the power dynamic in the legal sector. In part this may be true, but the entry of the Big Four is neither homogeneous, nor is it likely to be the sole driver of change to the way law is delivered.

There are a number of ways in which the Big Four present a meaningful threat to all law firms.

One area where the Big Four stands out amongst legal clients is their brand strength. In a marketplace where procurement and technology are driving change, and law firms readily acknowledge that the power of personal relationships is diminishing, having a strong brand with a solid reputation is essential.

But the advantage of the Big Four doesn't stop there. A significant barrier for all law firms, large and small, is the ability to access capital investment. For the Big Four, access to capital is seemingly easy. For example, in August of 2018, EY announced[5] an eye-watering commitment to spend US$1 billion on new technology, client service, and investment. Add to this the deep experience of the Big Four in implementing technology systems, and one can see further challenges for mid-sized law firms.

A final advantage for the Big Four is their ability to innovate. With no historic or cultural legacy hampering innovation and no need to placate an existing large lawyer-based partnership, the Big Four can think out of the box. The recent purchase by EY of the Pangea3 legal managed services business from Thomson Reuters[6] shows how EY is able to think about legal services in a manner that for most law firms would be incomprehensible. Through this purchase, EY is looking to advise corporations on how to drive greater efficiency in the delivery of in-house legal services, to the detriment of their external legal service providers.

Big Law performing

According to the 2019 Citi-Hildebrand Report,[7] the general economic performance of US law firms saw a strong 6.3 percent growth rate. Yet the data masks an underlying challenge for mid-sized law firms. Much of that growth, according to the study, came from the Top 50 law firms.

Undoubtedly some of the growth in the AmLaw 100 came from the continued trend towards market consolidation, as well as increased activity in lateral hires. However, probably more importantly was the increasing realization amongst the top firms that the status quo is no longer an option, hence a movement to adopt new management approaches, new technology innovation to drive future success. Consequently, the ability of these Big Law firms to think differently is yet another wake-up call for mid-sized law firms.

That said, the Citi-Hildebrand report was not all doom and gloom. In fact, there is arguably a bright future for mid-sized firms who grasp the opportunity that comes in change. As the report noted:

> *Performance often depends on which law firms have most successfully branded and built their reputations. In the case of niche firms, many strong performers "are those firms that have become very well known for what they do..." And while demand fell for the majority of Second Hundred firms, a select group significantly outperformed their direct peers, the Am Law 100, and niche practice rivals: 15 percent of Second Hundred firms had a growth rate of 5 percent or higher.*

What does this all mean for mid-sized law firms?

As noted, the overall picture is not all doom and gloom and, arguably for mid-sized law firms, the solutions may be easier to achieve than for their Big Law Competitors. Additionally, many of the solutions don't require deep pockets, an over-reliance on technology, or a dogmatic commitment to innovation. Instead, they require mid-sized law firms to understand who they are and what makes them successful, while embracing new management approaches and being diligent in the implementation of these approaches. That said, change will not come without challenges and it will require these firms to operate at a new level of sophistication and place new demands on their partners.

Hope is not a strategy

As noted in the introduction, there will be many winners and losers in the legal sector of the future. As the Citi-Hildebrand study highlighted, 30 firms in the second 100 of US law firms are already winning by posting growth rates greater than 5 percent. In many cases those firms are blending the best of what differentiates them, empowering their leaders to make the necessary changes, all while harnessing their lower cost structures.

Despite the increasing sophistication of law firms at all levels, it still seems that many law firms don't have a clear, concise business and market strategy. And of those that do, many find it difficult to consistently implement their strategy. Additionally, according to the Center of the Legal Profession at Harvard Law School,[8] "Most law firms continue to plan for short-term incremental improvements, deferring long term future-oriented strategies".

For mid-sized law firms there is a unique opportunity to take their smaller partnership size, closer interpersonal relations, and proximity to their clients and shape a strategy. But strategy development does require some tough management decisions. Making the tough decisions isn't easy. According to a recent survey by Altman Weil,[9] 69 percent of law firm partners resist most change efforts. However, there are a few simple but effective things that mid-sized law firms can do.

Firstly, speak to your clients. They will help you understand what you are known for, what you are good at, and what areas you need to improve. They will also help you understand where future industry, practice, and market growth is likely to come from.

Secondly, use independent measures of success – most notably your financial data set – to help shape your priorities. And then integrate partner inputs to create a holistic plan. This plan should also create a benchmark that is vital to evaluate ongoing performance. It is no surprise that the Big Four, with their number crunching accountancy legacy, are strong at evaluating their performance against plan. Making this a central aspect of your planning process ensures you are further ahead than most of your legal market competitors.

Thirdly, make sure you spend as much time embedding your strategic plan as you do creating it. Most plans fail because they are shelved, only to be dusted off at the end of the year to help prepare next year's plan. If you can embed quarterly deep dive strategic reviews, you will be significantly ahead of most of your competition.

Finally, recognize that strategic development can be complex, time-consuming and difficult. It's an ongoing process that cannot be ignored. But you can avoid some of the pain by firstly shaping out a set of longer term (three to five year) objectives that ideally won't change, and then plan on annual cycles. This means that once you've been through the pain of the first year, subsequent years should become easier.

Collaboration is a virtue

In my close to 15 years advising Big Four firms, including a number as a Big Four chief marketing officer, as well as the past seven years as the global chief marketing officer for one of the world's largest law firms, the challenge of driving client-focused partner collaboration has always been at the forefront of how to create lasting success.

But collaboration is not just a nice thing to do. In an increasingly competitive marketplace, it is essential. As clients become more sophisticated, they are less willing to tolerate a lack of collaboration between partners. These clients understand the need for both deep expertise, combined with holistic client solutions, if for no other reason than to drive efficiency. For law firm revenues, the importance of collaboration is paramount.

An increasing number of client studies show that having multiple practices working on a client not only increases client "stickiness" – the willingness of a client to work with firms through challenges – but also triples client revenues. In my own experience as a CMO of a Big Four firm, we had a rule of thumb that a key client (one with more than three practices working for them) should expect to see revenue growth at least twice the rate of the relevant industry sector.

The first essential step to driving revenue-oriented collaboration is the recognition that clients want partners to collaborate. It makes their lives easier having partners help solve their problems, which also mitigates managing multiple law firm relationships.

Secondly, partner collaboration is not only helpful to the top and bottom line, it is also helpful to building a stronger firm culture.

Thirdly, management needs to establish collaboration in action as well as words – thereby working with the finance department to build an internal accounting structure to track cross practice and/or cross regional referrals.

Fourthly, take the financial data and use it to reward top collaborators. Not just in terms of revenue but in term of client introductions.

Finally, recognize that partners may have legitimate concerns about introducing fellow partners into a well established, well functioning client relationship. Concerns about whether or not partners will respect their relationship with the client, or about the competency of a newly introduced group, need to be managed. This is where firm leadership needs the managerial authority to ensure all parties, including the client, are well represented. Because, if done well, the benefits of collaboration are well established.

Thank heaven for managing partners

Few people who understand what's going on in the legal sector would say it's an easy time to be in law firm leadership. Whether it be procurement-led purchasing, the advent of AI-led technology solutions, multi-million-dollar technology investments, or delivering successful full firm mergers, the myriad of new challenges for managing partners would have seemed unfathomable less than five years ago. Yet, given the complexity of the role of the managing partner, few firms have evolved in how they empower their leaders to be successful.

Amongst Big Law there have been movements to professionalize this role by bringing in outside CEOs who are not necessarily lawyers, while the Big Four have spent years perfecting a management rotation system that moves partners through management functions before they become a managing partner or CEO.

For mid-sized law firms without deep pockets there is a need to create a model that is both responsive to the partnership while still enabling the managing partner to act independently. For some firms this means moving away from an environment where the managing partner is limited to the role of consensus builder with limited strategic power, or others where managing partners are lifetime appointments with little prospect of bringing in fresh thinking through leadership change.

Taking a leaf from other partnership organizations means adopting new approaches.

Firstly, create term limits. Two four-year terms ensures the managing partner is responsive to the partnership to ensure a second term but has long enough to deliver against strategic priorities.

Second, this model can only be truly successful if the firm gives the managing partner a soft landing, an entry back into the firm as a revenue generating leader, or the firm's support in securing board appointments that ensure the professional and financial security of the individual in question. This is the approach taken by the Big Four as term-limited managing partners are given other responsibilities within the firm, or, with the firm's assistance, secure lucrative board appointments.

Additionally, firm leadership needs partner support to address the new market dynamics by bringing on non-lawyer professional talent – be that a chief financial officer, chief marketing officer or chief technology officer. With limited investment pools at the disposal of the managing partner, these hires understandably need to fit into the strategic plan.

Finally, as the managing partner builds out this team, it is essential that the firms build a culture of accountability for its professional staff, while at the same time ensuring they get the professional respect they deserve.

If mid-sized law firm managing partners are able to secure the support of their partners to think about the long-term challenges they face, have the time and permission to implement real change and hire professionals that have the support of their partnership, they will go a long way to out-compete their Big Law competitors.

What has technology ever done for me?

One of the undoubted challenges for all law firms is determining what technologies to invest in, how to secure the necessary capital for investment, and – probably most importantly – ensuring that the investment is not wasted.

In a market environment where members of the Big Four have committed to spend a billion dollars on technology and innovation (and reportedly[10] members of Big Law have individually committed to spend numbers around $60 million) it is not surprising the mid-sized law firms are looking at technology with fear and trepidation. However, one thing that is nearly universal – most technology implementations fail to realize their full expectations. In fact, reports[11] suggest that 25 percent of technology projects fail outright, 20-25 percent don't show any return on investment, and as much as 50 percent need massive reworking by the time they're finished. Add to this research[12] that shows that 68 percent of lawyers resist change and the picture for all those Big Law tech investments doesn't look very rosy.

However, for mid-sized law firms all this failure presents a huge competitive opportunity. Firstly, the data suggests that it is not the amount of money that one has to spend, but how wisely one spends it. Secondly, don't get caught up in the large figures associated with the capital investment and forget the vital operational spend. Thirdly, adhere to the adage of "fail fast".

All this failure with technology implementation is not an excuse to avoid technology investment. Remember, well over 50 percent of CLOC survey respondents are investing in technology solutions to manage their legal work. These clients expect that law firms will be investing in similar technologies to deliver more efficient, high quality service. In fact, by listening to clients and building a strong technology focus into the strategic plan, one can compete with the larger firms.

It's all about the clients

A final area in which mid-sized law firms can out-compete Big Law is by listening to their clients and taking client feedback seriously. While the Big Four have put in place rigorous client listening initiatives, Big Law has not embraced this concept wholeheartedly. Far too often partners are able to limit organized firm activity to secure client feedback on how they are being serviced and overall perceptions of the firm itself.

One way that Big Four firms have overcome partner opposition to client feedback is to have a simple three strike rule. Plainly put, a partner can effectively opt their client out of a client listening survey on two occasions in a two-year period. However, there is no limitation upon the firm's third attempt to elicit client feedback.

However, even more important than securing client input regarding the firm's service is building a culture whereby clients really are at the core of all aspects of how the firm operates. Remarkably this places firms who do this well far above their competition, large or small.

Conclusion

In a hyper-competitive legal market, many industry commentators have started to write off mid-sized law firms in terms of their ability to compete against the Big Four, Big Law and the rise of technology. However, by harnessing a small number of actions, including embedding a clear strategy, making client-oriented partner collaboration the core of service delivery, ensuring managing partners have the necessary structure and support to lead the firm, operationalizing smart technology investment and putting clients first, these firms have a clear opportunity to thrive as one of the winners of the future of law.

References

1. www.altmanweil.com/LFiT2018/
2. www.brainyquote.com/quotes/bill_gates_404193
3. https://blog.lawgeex.com/lawgeex-launches-2018-legal-technology-buyers-guide-for-in-house-counsel/
4. https://cloc.org/wp-content/uploads/2019/07/2019-State-of-the-Industry-FINAL.pdf
5. www.ey.com/en_gl/news/2018/08/ey-to-spend-us-1-billion-as-part-of-its-innovation-drive
6. www.ey.com/en_gl/news/2019/06/ey-announces-completion-of-pangea3-legal-managed-services-acquisition
7. www.privatebank.citibank.com/home/fresh-insight/citi-hildebrandt-clientadvisory.html
8. https://thepractice.law.harvard.edu/article/steering-law-firm-strategy/
9. www.altmanweil.com/LFiT2018/
10. www.ey.com/en_gl/news/2018/08/ey-to-spend-us-1-billion-as-part-of-its-innovation-drive
11. www.forbes.com/sites/bernardmarr/2016/09/13/are-these-the-real-reasons-why-tech-projects-fail/#553a296b7320
12. www.altmanweil.com/LFiT2018/

Chapter 5: The Janus challenge

By Nancey Watson, president of NL Watson Consulting Inc

The ancient Roman god IANVS (Jānus) is usually depicted as having two faces, since he looks to the future and to the past. Big Law, mid-sized firms, small firms and boutiques have advantages and challenges built on the past and looking into the future.

The expression "one-size-fits-all" does not apply to law firms. They come in all shapes and sizes – large, medium, small, or boutique and national, regional, or local. Depending upon what a client or potential employee is looking for will determine where the law firm fits. Size and structure will often dictate important factors such as culture, compensation, practice areas, types of clients, how decisions are made with regard to management, client representation, and business strategy.

I have worked with all kinds of law firms and can say that they are all very different. Not only within their peer group but also compared to different size firms. Each has a place in today's marketplace. This chapter discusses firms of various sizes and strengths and how they can put themselves in the position to win more business and effectively compete in various markets by virtue of focusing on various levels of quality and/or service and delivery models.

Big Law

Big Law is considered to provide full legal services. They cater to a variety of legal practices and offer highly experienced lawyers. They are usually national or global in geographical scope.

Working for a large law firm versus a medium-size or boutique firm can be compared to living in a big city versus the countryside. Neither is right or wrong, it all depends upon what is preferred or needed.

Due to the nature of legal matters, Big Law will always be needed to handle complex cases. The issue is more a matter of which firms will be selected to perform the work. As business becomes more complex and the transactions become bigger there is always going to be a need for the big guns. Increasingly though, Big Law is adopting different ways to operate and become more competitive with the inclusion of legal operations teams.

Many are the advantages of Big Law, the biggest draw being to have the opportunity to specialize in complex and sophisticated areas of practice and lawyers who are recognized by the industry for their expertise in the field. They offer services locally and internationally so the opportunities to service global firms would be of interest for those looking for challenges on an international scale.

Benefits of Big Law:

- Legal expertise and reputation;
- Higher salaries and better benefits;
- Large and diversified client base;
- Resources e.g. libraries and support staff;
- Promotions as positions open up and global transfers;
- Robust CLE training and mentoring programs; and
- Advanced technology and training.

Challenges of Big Law:

- Long hours and billable hour requirements;
- Mundane tasks for junior lawyers, e.g. document review;
- Formal corporate culture;
- Less personalized contact with clients; and
- Big organizations are slow to change.

Mid-sized firms

Mid-sized firms can put themselves in a position to win more business and effectively compete in various markets. The Big Four and Big Law have a number of approaches to their positioning, marketing, and business development that have effectively differentiated them from many of their competitors and therefore put them on the road to success. For mid-sized firms there are a number of approaches that can be incorporated into their marketing and business development that will help them be successful.

That said, they can also develop their own strategies for market success that, if implemented effectively, mean they can out-compete Big Law. If mid-sized firms grasp the basics, develop a coherent strategy, and implement that strategy with focus and daily vigilance, they can ensure they not only thrive, but that they prosper in this time of change.

Mid-sized firms are in a good situation because they are in a top position in certain markets; many have a geographical niche and practice offerings that fit with the local economy. It is unlikely that Big Law will settle in a smaller community like Baton Rouge so the competition from large law firms is much lower for local firms in smaller areas.

Richard Brzakala, director of external legal services at a large Canadian financial institution, an expert in legal operations with over 20 years of experience managing and interacting with hundreds of law firms of all shapes and sizes around the world, confirms that:

> *"Mid-sized firms (for start-up and Big Business clients) are more affordably priced than Big Law firms. I believe that most clients are attracted to mid-sized firms primarily because of their expertise and experience as it relates to a specific business sector (e.g. agriculture, mining, fishery, indigenous rights), practice group or geographic location (e.g. cross border, state, or provincial). They are increasingly becoming a challenge to Big Law, as their pricing structure is significantly lower and more cost effective than Big Law's. In fact, I have repeatedly seen Big Law leveraging mid-sized firms, as co-counsel on large corporate transactions or for local (regional) litigation expertise. Their increased popularity with Big Business has also made mid-sized firms attractive takeover targets for Big Law firms who are looking to scale up their operations in lucrative practice or geographical areas."*

Mid-sized law firms provide an opportunity that Big Law does not because they are not as siloed and can offer more breadth of experience to their associates. The training model where associates are mentored by an experienced lawyer is still economically viable in mid-sized firms, more so than in large firms due to their business model. New lawyers are typically given tasks that encompass entire projects, not just pieces of a large project. Therefore, they see the big picture and understand the client's needs. Building a rapport with clients is one of the great things about being a lawyer and associates get exposure to working with clients sooner.

Many clients are now refusing to pay for associates with fewer than two to three years of experience. The pyramid structure and pricing model of many large law firms is not conducive to this model. A mid-sized firm is more flexible and the pricing structure can accommodate lower pricing options.

Mid-sized firms are also able to make changes quickly as they have less bureaucracy. They can make adjustments to compensation, remote working policies, IT expenditures and marketing programs on a dime because they have a small trusted group of partners, or just one, who makes the final decisions. This is a great advantage over Big Law as, the bigger they are, the more layers they need to go through for approval.

There is also an opportunity for a different kind of lifestyle that an increasing number of millennials are drawn to, in particular a preference for work–life balance. Not all graduates want to work for Big Law or in a big city. Mid-sized firms have fewer lawyers and develop close ties with their fellow lawyers. As the practice is smaller they know their colleagues, practice areas, and clients. I work for Big Law and Big Four accounting firms and am frequently asked who I would recommend in another office or practice area to participate in a proposal – this is because I know the lawyers better than many of the lawyers participating on a proposal, because I have worked with so many of them on different bids. It is understandable that local lawyers cannot be well acquainted with 8,000+ employees globally.

Mid-sized firms are in the enviable position of having the mid-market business. This is the growth sector of the economy. Big Law is unable to convince medium-sized and small businesses that they can afford them. After all, there are only 500 "Fortune 500" companies and the pie is already split up. Large law firms have set up special departments with special rates to attract this growing market but have not been terribly successful. I remember the Big Four acquired mid-sized accounting firms for this very reason. Big Law now has emerging tech companies on its radar as these are quickly becoming very profitable enterprises. Mid-sized firms need to protect their turf and look at new areas of business.

Benefits of mid-sized:

- Mid-market clients;
- Can out-price Big Law;
- Opportunity to work with clients sooner;
- Strong personal touch;

- More balanced lifestyle;
- Promotions in a less competitive environment;
- Variety of work – end-to-end; and
- Flexible, can implement changes more quickly.

Challenges of mid-sized:

- Lower salaries and fewer benefits;
- Less sophisticated technology and R&D;
- Fewer support staff and specialists, e.g. pricing and legal project management; and
- Fewer formalized processes.

Small firms

Smaller and more local firms usually represent smaller or middle-market clients in smaller, less complex matters because they do not have the resources to staff large, complex cases. These firms can be structured in a similar way to larger firms, or boutique firms. Small firms suit those who like to be a "big fish in a small pond". This is possible because there are fewer lawyers to spread the work around, coupled with the opportunity to work more closely with senior lawyers. These firms compete with their peers and need to differentiate themselves in the marketplace. They need to identify their service offerings (faster, better, less expensive) and expertise (awards) just like any other kind of law firm. I find it interesting that I am often the one who points out the differentiators to my clients – it is like the old forest-for-the-trees scenario.

Benefits of a small firm:

- Varied work and experience;
- Client interaction at an earlier stage;
- More informal atmosphere;
- Know senior lawyers better;
- Openness to change; and
- Flatter management structure.

Challenges for small firms:

- Lower salaries;
- Limited resources;
- Impact of market fluctuations;
- Professional isolation; and
- Lack of innovative technology.

Boutiques

A boutique firm's lawyers specialize in one niche area of practice. Although most mid-sized and large law firms have structured themselves to offer a broad range of services, boutiques can tout themselves as specialists in a particular area of law, such as intellectual property (IP), immigration, or commercial litigation and the defence of SEC investigations, thus gaining an enviable reputation in certain markets. Some boutiques also specialize in certain industries such as pharmaceutical and energy. I particularly enjoy working with boutique firms because there is an interesting mix of lawyers. For example, IP firms typically have lawyers with MBAs and PhDs in science, chemistry, and engineering. This makes for interesting dynamics when responding to RFPs.

Evan J Green, managing partner of a Toronto immigration boutique, states that:

> *"Due to the fact that immigration law is fluid, it is always changing, a lawyer cannot dabble in the field and do it well. You need to do it all the time to be really good at it. That is where we excel. Our track record gives clients a great deal of comfort knowing that we are not experimenting with their case. We are a small firm, our clients know that they can call us, can count on us, and we will be there for them."*

Boutique law firms are now showing up on the global scene; for example, law firms in Asia are enticing business away from general practice firms. The transfer from large law firms to mid-sized to boutiques is driven by a need to reduce costs and to obtain the services of recognized lawyers with specialized experience. As business becomes more complex this trend is likely to continue.

Boutiques are often the target of Big Law mergers as they have an established reputation and client base in areas of law that can be quite lucrative. The opposite is also true where practice areas of Big Law firms break off and create their own boutiques. There is never a dull moment in the ever-changing legal industry.

Benefits of a boutique firm:

- Highly specialized lawyers;
- Referral business when experts are required;
- Client interaction at all levels;
- More informal atmosphere; and
- Less hierarchy.

Challenges for a boutique firm:

- Limited resources;
- Impact of market fluctuations;
- Professional isolation;
- Lack of innovative technology; and
- More likely to hire only experienced lawyers.

Each kind of law firm has its benefits and challenges. It is important for firms to recognize the differences when they strategize their business development and marketing campaigns. There is a place for everyone at this time but that doesn't mean that your area of expertise or geographical advantage won't be under attack in the future. Sometimes to determine what lies in the future requires us to look behind to uncover the evolution of our firms and our market niche and root out the bad and exploit the good. Success will come to those who employ the Janus challenge.

Chapter 6:
Mid-sized law firms – competitive and innovation strategies

By Mark Medice, principal, LawVision LLC

In today's environment, mid-sized law firms are in a unique position to compete. Some view this segment as being challenged in scale, footprint, and the ability to afford the latest technological capabilities. Others see the challenges as opportunities – an agile, fleetfooted group that can provide tailored services with a strong personal touch and exploit mid-sized scale to be more responsive and tuned-in to the clients they wish to serve, using new approaches to the practice.

In this chapter, Mark Medice, principal with LawVision who works with law firms on strategy, innovation, data analytics, and financial performance, interviews four managing partners from forward-looking mid-sized firms about their strategies, thoughts on innovation, how they think about the competitive marketplace, managing change to transform their practices, along with their views on data and other technologies changing the practice.

The participants in the discussion included:

Marci A Eisenstein, managing partner, Schiff Hardin LLP

Marci Eisenstein is the managing partner of Schiff Hardin LLP. She has spent the last 30 years defending major corporations against more than 100 class action challenges in federal and state courts nationwide and is one of few lawyers in the country to try a nationwide consumer class action to verdict. When Marci was elected managing partner in 2015, she became the first woman to hold this top post in the firm's 150-year history. Under her leadership, Schiff Hardin was twice named an "Illinois Powerhouse" firm by *Law360* in 2018 and 2019. Marci remains among only a handful of female managing partners in Big Law firms across the United States.

Schiff Hardin LLP is a law firm of nearly 300 lawyers, having grown from one office to seven over 150 years. As a general practice firm, Schiff

Hardin has strong capabilities in most legal disciplines and a total dedication to client service.

Jeffrey S Sharp, managing partner, Marshall, Gerstein & Borun LLP
Jeffrey S Sharp is the managing partner of Marshall, Gerstein & Borun LLP. He is a registered patent attorney with more than 30 years of experience in patent prosecution, litigation and transactional work who focuses his practice in the areas of biotechnology, chemistry, and chemical engineering. Jeffrey has handled matters in a wide variety of biotechnology disciplines, such as pharmaceuticals, nutraceuticals, and gene therapy; recombinant nucleic acid technologies, including plant biotechnology; and in-vivo and in-vitro diagnostic and gene-sequencing methods. He has also gained successful outcomes in diverse chemical and chemical engineering technologies, including organic, inorganic, and metallurgical chemistry; chemical and metallurgical processing; and food and beverage chemistry.

Marshall, Gerstein & Borun LLP provides sophisticated intellectual property advice and legal services to many of the world's largest, most innovative businesses, research institutions, universities, and entrepreneurs. For more than six decades, the firm has been exclusively dedicated to excellence in the practice of IP law. Its singular focus enhances efficiency, fosters responsive and creative decision-making, and helps clients achieve mission-critical results.

David Krutz, managing partner, Michael Best and Friedrich LLP
Over the past ten years, David has been instrumental in Michael Best's growth into a national presence from its Midwest base. While the firm has expanded to more than 300 lawyers and professionals who perform sophisticated work on a broad basis, Michael Best's core principles, including strong client partnerships and an entrepreneurial approach fueled by the spirit of collaboration, remain intact. David aims to ensure a continued commitment to the firm's core values as it moves forward along a trajectory of growth and change.

Michael Best is a full-service firm with offices in six states plus Washington, DC. It has a strong emphasis on intellectual property, corporate work for middle market and emerging businesses, employment and benefits, litigation, and regulatory areas such as energy, agribusiness, and government relations.

Robert Romanoff, chairman and managing partner, Levenfeld Pearlstein

Robert Romanoff is the chairman and managing partner of Levenfeld Pearlstein, LLC. In addition to his leadership role in the firm, Rob is a Chambers-rated estate planning attorney and a fellow in the American College of Trust and Estate Counsel.

Levenfeld Pearlstein is a 70-attorney firm with offices in Chicago and Northbrook, Illinois. The firm was created in 1999, born of the desire to create a different kind of law firm. The firm employs a client-centric business strategy (The LP Way™) as its model for creating an unparalleled client experience at an exceptional value. Client service is the motivation behind all actions and systems put into place at LP.

Mark Medice is a principal at LawVision and leads the financial performance and data science practice. He has over 20 years of leadership experience, providing and applying data solutions to the most pressing challenges facing law firm leaders. Mark spent over ten years at Thomson Reuters where he launched and led the Peer Monitor program. During that time, he created the Peer Monitor Index (PMI) which is widely used throughout the legal industry. Immediately prior to LawVision, Mark led new initiatives around analytics and metrics at Intapp. He began his legal career in-house at Procter & Gamble and was an associate with Morgan Lewis.

Background and market segmentation

Mark: The industry for the delivery of legal services is quite different today than it was 10 or 20 years ago. A very large firm was once thought to be 500 to 1,000 lawyers but now we see firms at 10,000 lawyers, not to mention alternative Big Four providers operating at an entirely different scale. What is a mid-sized firm today?

Robert Romanoff: Our firm operates with a strong commitment to a service philosophy that depends on being a certain size. We have 70 lawyers, all of whom know each other. Our model operates with service levels that match our size and it provides a competitive advantage. Part of the mid-sized model requires an acknowledgement that your firm does not provide every area of service.

Marci A Eisenstein: The definition of a mid-sized firm has grown relative to market changes. The industry has and will continue to experience consolidation. A mid-sized firm today might be thought of as being upwards of 700 lawyers, which when you think about it is a sizable large firm. We have half a dozen offices and 300 lawyers as a mid-sized firm.

Jeffrey S Sharp: Our firm is a full-spectrum intellectual property firm. To us, our scale of 90 specialists focused on intellectual property is a strategic choice and our size allows us to operate with a strategy that enables us to serve our clients with focused distinction.

David Krutz: We have four offices in Wisconsin and seven outside the state centered around growing markets and technology centers such as Denver, Salt Lake City, Raleigh and Austin. We have developed strong practices in Chicago and Washington DC. Beyond the core practices of intellectual property, corporate, employment and litigation, we target specific industries and specialty areas in new markets. I agree with other commentators about the characteristics of mid-sized firms. We believe we operate as a true partnership, and not just having someone be a partner in name only. Once a firm grows to a certain size, many intimacies of partnership can be lost.

Mark: Maybe just counting lawyers is not the right way to segment the firms in their entirety. Part of the way you want to practice, service clients, and specialize plays a role.

Robert: How all the pieces of size, service and strategy fit together are essential to how the firm operates.

Marci: The way we compensate people is not formulaic. We really know who our people are and understand their practices. Our lawyers value that highly and so do our clients. They know we bring to market the quality of people we can vouch for and stand behind.

Mark: Is the mid-sized segment threatened by changes in the marketplace – whether it be due to very large firms consolidating, new competitors coming into the market, or the need to invest in technologies at a pace not seen before?

David: Viability goes to practice areas and often geography. There is a need for a certain amount of depth in most practice areas to compete for top level work. Without that depth, you may not be able to compete. How much breadth you have as a firm depends on what size you are willing to go. That is why I appreciate what Marci said when she says she considers her firm to be mid-sized. The other thing I would point to is that at the top of the "food chain," for example international M&A and corporate deals, many GCs and board of directors are looking for certain branded firm names. The reality is that many of those transactions will not be for mid-sized firms.

Marci: The other question involves infrastructure and economies of scale. A large firm can achieve economies of scale in technology and real estate, and by pursuing strategies like back offices in inexpensive locations. On the other hand, we don't have the bureaucracy, and we can harness our own intellectual capital more effectively.

Jeff: I would also point out the conflicts challenges that exist as you get larger and more spread out. For very large litigation matters we find that we are able to co-counsel with other firms and bring more resources to bear and that sometimes works well with clients.

Marci: A lot of laterals come to us because on a relative basis we can offer a better conflict-free zone, and that gives the lawyers more freedom.

Competitive threats from other segments

Mark: What about alternative providers or larger law firms? How threatening are these competitors?

Robert: I don't spend a lot of time worrying about it – we do have clients with a global reach and have partnered with affiliate firms and that has worked well for us. But this isn't central to our strategy. We typically do not represent multi-national companies and so it isn't directly hitting us in the markets in which we serve.

Marci: One major client approached us and other outside firms, some of which were significantly larger than our firm, wanting us to work with them in a particular way outside the traditional law firm model. The proposal involved lawyers servicing the client full-time and operating on a cost-plus basis. Compared to other firms, we were able to be more flexible in partnering with them. That enabled us to deepen the relationship more effectively than the other larger firms serving the client. The larger firms were not sufficiently flexible to consider changes to their model.

David: I take a different approach on the competitive threat. I look at the history of our home state of Wisconsin for example. Twenty or even

15 years ago, if there was a major corporate merger, transaction, or litigation, we would have been on the shortlist for the entity doing work in Wisconsin because of our presence in the state. Today, with more and more law firms having a multi-state presence and the use of technology, it is no longer a guarantee that we will be part of those transactions. Rather, we have to compete for the work. In short, there is an incremental chipping away at the market from outside law firms. The future threat is that if international law firms or accounting firms bring more formal business and controlled processes that drive efficiency and lower their price, we could lose what we think is our current pricing advantage. I do view the idea of larger, highly efficient firms as a significant competitive threat over the next five years.

Mark: What you are describing is like the sound of marketplace disruption where the threat appears to be incremental but accelerates before incumbents realize fully what is going on. Do you see your firms as materially larger over the next five years, whether that is measured by timekeepers, offices, technology or any other measure?

Jeff: We see steady growth depending on the needs of our clients, probably to the order of five percent annually. We are a full-service IP firm and are constantly marketing but have no active plans to push our growth beyond our current service levels within our current markets. We look at growth in the context of serving the needs of our existing and prospective clients.

Marci: Same approach for us.

David: We are in strategic planning right now. I anticipate a heavy emphasis on technology, alternative staffing models, and new professional roles such as data analytics – something akin to our engineer model.[1] We want to produce high quality legal work, but with a reduced cost model. It is hard to compete for recent law school graduates in some of our markets where law students are coming out and making almost $200,000 per year in base salary. We are focusing on steady growth but, revenue and service-wise, we are looking to supplement our attorney growth through alternative talent and technology.

Jeff: I agree with that. Like David's firm we make heavy use of technical specialists and patent agents.

Robert: My answer would be slightly different. We have invested very heavily in paralegals. We don't have the engineers that Michael Best has but we have a corps of paralegals much larger than firms of our size. I would like to be able to offer the same answer as others in terms of controlled growth, but we have added 14 lawyers in the past year, and we are still a fairly young firm. We have seen the emergence of our younger partners in developing business and we see our growth as inextricably tied to meeting our clients' needs.

Changes to the business model and innovation

Mark: Getting into change and doing things differently, we have talked already about things you are doing, and the advantages/disadvantages mid-sized firms may have. Can you provide examples of things you are doing that represent meaningful change to service delivery, innovation, or client service?

Robert: Our change has primarily focused on P3: process improvement, project management, and pricing. Really looking at how we can reengineer the work we do and reduce the amount of time we spend on matters. Every year we train our lawyers in Lean Six Sigma training. All our lawyers are trained at least as white belts and we have others at higher levels. In 2012, we brought into the firm a manager of process improvement. At the same time, we looked critically at our pricing functions to change how we charge. We continue to be heavily focused on that area.

Mark: Is that translating into any quantitative measurement – improved margin growth, premium prices, better alignment with value? What outcomes are you seeing?

Robert: I think in specific areas there has been a direct correlation to increased profitability. My area in trusts and estates is a good example of that. I think it also has been helpful in helping our lawyers understand the word "value". The traditional model has been for lawyers to measure value by the number of billable hours. It has been helpful in the past several years for lawyers to see that value is determined by the client, and meeting or exceeding that standard is the objective. People in our firm and in the industry are becoming much more sensitized to tying value to the client.

Mark: Is counting billable hours something you still do for purposes of lawyer reward or recognition?

Robert: The answer is no. We moved away from the billable hour model seven years ago. All of our dashboards are tied to revenue because when we tied production measurement to the billable hour, that is exactly what we got. Getting more hours with lower realization is not a strategy we employ. We still track hours in order to measure utilization, chargeable hours, and investment time. We want our attorneys to manage their time, and we track their time to help manage it. We still have lawyers who think in terms of billable hours, so it is an effort that continues.

Marci: Our clients generally don't want to be billed by the hour. We are looking at the billable hour but are much more focused on profitability. Given the number of fee caps and fixed fees we are doing, we are much more focused on efficiency and results over hours. We regularly explore ways to consistently provide client value and deliver legal services more effectively.

Jeff: Thirty to 40 percent of our work is fixed fees as we do significant amounts of patent and trademark prosecution work as a full-service IP firm. We still track hours for this work but do that for cost accounting and profitability calculations and to understand efficiency in resource allocation. We have many technical specialists and patent agents. We are still hiring lawyers but doing strategic hiring of technical specialists, some but not all of whom go to law school.

Mark: Jeff, are your new talent roles as effective as the roles they are replacing, for example, a lawyer?

Jeff: Absolutely. The price differential is significant and if someone has been a patent agent for say five years, their efficiency upon graduating from law school and becoming a first-year associate is really high. This works out really well for our clients and for the firm.

Mark: You folks specialize in the area of intellectual property but today the market value of the body of services can have cost differentials. How are you handling that?

Jeff: We have a highly trained legal assistant staff that operate like paralegals. We have not been pushing our secretarial staff to lawyer ratio too much because our legal assistants make our lawyers super-efficient. We are focusing on refining our work processes which involve both people and technology, but we have a fantastic secretarial staff.

Marci: We are looking at how to make our operations more efficient. Some of the things we are examining include a higher lawyer to secretarial ratio, creating role specialization, as well as looking at a staff attorney model where staff lawyers can be supervised by partners to meet the needs of clients. The objective is to address the legal delivery service model. We want to have our lawyers focus on the premise that value is determined by the client, and the client wants us to deliver the work to them more efficiently. That has to be our mantra.

David: We focus our reporting on partner production on revenue generation, including working receipts, matters managed, and client originations. We do not stress utilization (or billable hours) for partners. For associates, we have decreased the amount of bonus dollars available based on billable hours. Associate bonuses used to be a straight billable hour model. We now have three tiers of associates – junior, middle, and senior class. There is a cap on bonuses based on billable hours. Five years ago we recognized that we had lawyers wanting to be partners who were really good at billing hours but, as Robert said, it really is what you do with your investment time, as well as being good collaborators, being active in the market, doing charitable activities, or other things that represent the desired qualities of a partner. The billable hour target becomes less important. For example, when you are doing alternative fees you want to track billables to manage budgets, but we really want the lawyers focused on revenue and quality work performance rather than billable hours.

Mark: Importance of profitability has been raised a number of times. What are you doing and how important is it to you?

David: We have spent a lot of time on measuring profitability because of our practice mix, and the number of fixed fee arrangements we have. We break it down by client, matter, attorney, and team. We segment the results in quadrants. We focus on the lower quadrants and coach the partners on how to improve it. It does have an effect on their behavior. We give higher bonuses to those who have higher volume fees with corresponding high profitability. We inform the partners of the areas where we need to improve profitability. We are using profitability as a tool, and we would consider disengaging some clients if we do not have a mutually beneficial relationship in terms of fees.

Marci: We are focused on profitability as well and can slice-and-dice by lawyer, client, and practice group through various lenses. We are educating our partners on this. We are also encouraging them to staff those matters better, to take a different approach and be more effective and profitable at the same time. We have done a lot to get our people educated that not all our revenue is the same.

Jeff: What is useful to the lawyers is to know how the models work rather than using them blindly. If you don't understand how the models work they can drive the wrong kinds of behavior such as using lawyers who are already over-utilized rather than those who have capacity.

Robert: We have been focused on profitability for a long time. At the ARK Group Midsize Conference where we spoke together, our CMO and CFO showed a tool we use to educate lawyers on profitability. Profitability has to be tied to strategy. Be careful of gaming, like using the busy associate. We will sometimes see people using paralegals rather than associates to increase the profitability of matters but that is not in line with our client retention strategy. We want other attorneys involved for client succession and continuity. So we need to be careful not to be overly focused on short-term measures without balancing in the strategic context.

David: Robert brings up an excellent point, which is why we focus on the lower profitability quadrant when evaluating financial performance and doing our partner coaching.

Summary thoughts

Marci: It is critical having lawyers embrace change. It is either change or die but this is challenging because lawyers are deconstructionists and can find the flaw in any model, which makes our job harder. We have to be very open to change or we ensure our obsolescence.

Jeff: Change is hard for any law firm but being mid-sized gives us some advantages there. With smaller groups it can be easier to do innovative things and experiment more and move a culture.

David: I am an advocate for using separate service entities to supplement our growth. The strategic philosophy of providing special entities is that they allow us to provide different touchpoints and services in the business community outside of law but consistent with our legal practices. This allows us to develop competitive advantages even if we are not the same size as national or international firms. I also encourage the use of skilled business people to make business judgements and implement solutions. I believe professionals with these skills will be increasingly important because they can implement process changes and let the lawyers focus on lawyering.

Robert: Our strategy is to view everything through the prism of our clients' needs. Our size allows us to align all of our systems around the client experience and allows for a cultural commitment from all of our team members, not just from a select group. As long as we remain focused on placing our clients' needs first, we will be able to remain agile and meet whatever challenges come our way.

Reference

1. Michael Best has successfully hired engineers to supplement and work alongside lawyers for specialized intellectual property work.

Chapter 7:
Tools and tech – can technology help level the playing field?

By Anand Upadhye, VP business development, Casetext

Introduction

It is evident to any industry insider that there are more legal technology products now than there have ever been. From e-discovery, to legal research, to analytics, to contract review, every niche and utility in legal is being addressed by legal tech companies. This explosion of available technology has created unprecedented opportunities for mid-sized firms. It also poses a threat to firms that choose to disregard this rise of innovation or merely acquire "shelfware", or technology that remains proverbially shrink-wrapped on a law firm shelf and un-adopted years after purchase. As clients demand more value for less, certain firms have leaned on technology to increase efficiency while maintaining accurate, high-caliber work product and minimizing risk, all while leveling the playing field with the largest law firms.

So how do you address these pressures without becoming disillusioned by the unending array of options and difficulties of technology adoption? To get a clearer picture, I reached out to some forward-thinking leaders at America's most innovative mid-sized and large law firms to learn from the best.

In our conversations, I asked two big questions: "What is your criterion for judging whether legal tech is good?" and "When you've brought it into the firm, how do you ensure that your attorneys will actually use it?"

I received a diverse array of responses on these topics from leaders at mid-sized firms such as Barnes & Thornburg, Allen Matkins, and Hinshaw & Culbertson, as well as large firms. While they all had unique insights from their extensive experience working with legal technology, we saw certain key themes emerge as it related to mid-sized firms. This chapter presents those ideas in the context of the two big questions.

These leaders shared perspectives and opinions from the worlds of knowledge management, pricing, the law library, firm innovation, and information technology. The experts generally referred to all types of legal technology, including contract review, legal research, and competitive intelligence.

The goal of this chapter is to provide you with ideas and guidance on how you can take advantage of your legal technology options and, after you've found technology that works, to assist you in planning a roll-out and adoption plan that entirely takes advantage of the newly purchased tech. While your firm may not be able to overwhelm the opposition with armies of attorneys staffed on every matter, you will be able to bring on strong technology that can be a force multiplier for each of your attorneys. Ultimately, good tech deployed well will deliver visible results in a relatively short period.

Part one – evaluating legal technology

In a marketplace saturated with options, it is daunting for legal technologists to do their due diligence in evaluating them, let alone mid-sized law firm professionals who are often juggling work done by a team of five at a larger firm. To understand how to approach the challenge of finding the most valuable tools for their firm, we asked our contributors:

What is your most important criterion when evaluating legal technology?

Several themes emerged in response to this broad question. I boiled it down to three key indicators to help you distinguish the useful from the useless.

Enterprise technology should look and feel like consumer technology

> "*[I]n law firms, enterprise technologies… are expected to function as smoothly as similar tools in their consumer lives.*" Vishal Agnihotri, chief knowledge officer at Hinshaw & Culbertson

Fifteen years ago, attorneys and information professionals were content with enterprise technology that looked like enterprise technology. It was unwieldy, required several hours of training, and the instruction manual was often intimidatingly long. Many professionals tolerated glitches, outages, and poor design, but times have changed. With the rise of the iPhone, Amazon, and other top-notch consumer technology, we've come to expect an intuitive user interface, high-quality design, and the ability to use the technology after only a brief tutorial (and no instruction manual).

This is arguably more critical to mid-sized and small firm professionals than any others. Large firms can afford to build teams of technology specialists to learn the ins and outs of unnecessarily complex software. They can offer in-person training and answer questions at all hours. This is unacceptable for more leanly staffed mid-sized law firm teams that simply cannot waste dozens or hundreds of hours a year on tedious training to often inattentive attorneys.

Lane Lowman, director of litigation support at Barnes & Thornburg, says:

> *"Apple has the right idea on this. Work hard to provide advanced technology and features but go the extra distance to make it easier to consume. I've seen very mature technology that is so complex that you can't remember how to run it. What good is it then?"*

Jason Nittel, director of litigation technology and support at Allen Matkins, observed that when it comes to legal technology:

> *"If attorneys design it, then they get it. If it was designed [only] by engineers, they don't understand what attorneys need."*

Vishal Agnihotri agreed that the firm looks for technology that "is constructed to withstand the above average critical scrutiny of a legal user".

Technology should be easy to learn, easy to use, and easy to explain. If it's not, you risk losing the interest of your attorneys, even if the tech is powerful. When you are assessing legal technology, ask: "Is this pleasant to use? If this wasn't 'law firm software', would I think it was well-designed and intuitive?"

Start with the business case, then look for the technology – not the other way around

Buy tools, not shiny objects associated with buzzwords. Frequently, legal technology vendors lead with appealing features, esoteric technologies, and futuristic claims of seamless automation. However, when you push away the slick marketing, the feature richness doesn't solve a real problem the firm is having. Agnihotri looks for product demonstrations and feedback from her attorneys that emphasizes the current use case:

> *"Instead of a feature-based approach, a useful legal technology would also lay out various use cases and examples of how it helps the lawyer in their day-to-day activities. Emphasize the usability of the tool."*

Other law firm leaders push back against meaningless buzzwords, frequently correlated with a vendor that is a "technology-first" company, uninterested with applied use cases. As Ali Shahidi, the chief innovation and client solutions officer at Sheppard Mullin puts it, "We like to get under the hood, simplify and demystify, especially when terms such as proprietary, intelligence and artificial are used in the same sentence".

Meredith Williams Range, chief knowledge and client solutions officer at Shearman & Sterling, focuses on not just the immediate use case, but the firm-wide business needs:

> *"We evaluate legal technology that serves a business need. It is not about just going after great technology. We evaluate the business need first by looking at profit margins, write-offs, and writedowns, etc. We then determine if the issue is people, process, tech, or data related. When tech is the issue, then we spend the time to evaluate the right set of solutions."*

Shahidi agrees: "We start with requirements and business priorities, to then identify solutions that are responsive to our attorneys' needs".

Mid-sized firm technology buyers attempting to buy slick tools and hope it finds a home in their attorneys' workflows are setting themselves up for failure. Building consensus on key attorney pain points, then searching for the right technology will give your firm the best chance to obtain technology that fits.

Find technology that will allow your attorneys to demonstrate value to the client

> *"It is critical to be in touch with your users and understand what tech will help them deliver legal services to clients."* Marlene Gebauer, Greenberg Traurig

With or without technology, clients have demanded the same thing for decades – high-quality, accurate work, done efficiently, with the client's business in mind. One of the ways mid-sized law firm attorneys demonstrate value to their clients is to employ technology that can mitigate risk. Extra points if the nature of the risk mitigation is clear and easy to communicate to the client.

In a sentiment echoed by many of her peers, Agnihotri said "[A tool needs to] mitigates risk for the lawyer or the firm or the client, because it flattens a process and reduces the compounding of errors that happens in multiple connected steps."

Part two – spurring usage and adoption

Selecting the best technologies is only half the battle; next comes the struggle of implementation. Our next question comes into play after the pitch, after the product evaluation, and after the contract is signed. I asked:

Why is new technology resisted at law firms? What have you done to overcome it?

Anyone who assumes that lawyers will automatically discover and loop the technology into their workflow is in for a big surprise. Our respondents advanced the three following suggestions for ensuring that your high-profile purchases make you a hero.

Partner with vendors you trust to roll-out and train your attorneys

> *"In addition to the technology review, we specifically give priority to those [technology providers] that can be collaborative partners through the engagement and adoption process."* Ali Shahidi

Shahidi advanced a theme that our panel of industry insiders fully backed – the era of law firms owning training, internal marketing, and technology engagement initiatives is in the rearview mirror. Lane Lowman, director of litigator support at Barnes & Thornburg, strongly agreed:

> *"Leverage your vendor to put articles of interest, news, upgrade notices, in front of your users. Get your attorneys constantly exposed to the benefits available. Using new technology and changing the way people do things does not come easy. You have to remain proactive and stay in front of them."*

Most law firms struggle to find the people resources and budget to perform their core duties as librarians, or information experts at the firm. The idea that they can break away for days at a time to design and execute on a firm-wide roll-out plan is unreasonable. Increasingly, legal technology companies are taking the laboring oar on everything from the logistics of providing access to the firm, to training, to engagement and ongoing education.

Leanly-run law firms should screen out vendors who are unwilling to invest in robust training, implementation, and support programs. The largest firms can protect against these deficiencies by allocating resources to do the vendor's job. Mid-sized firms do not have that luxury. Pre-negotiate a favorable training and support program, essentially off-loading critical work on the vendor, who may be better situated than your firm to provide it. As importantly, demand from your vendors that they design and execute on a plan tailored to your mid-sized firm.

Finally, create accountability from your vendors regarding metrics. With a baseline set, make it clear internally who is using the technology to increase efficiency and who is not. As Lowman suggests:

> *"We have tried several things to get our attorneys to use new technology. We have tried to keep people accountable by employing monthly usage reports that are shared by the entire user base. Everyone gets to see who is applying a new technology and who has done very little. We have then been willing to trade out the non-performers and give the opportunity to others."*

Approach your attorneys by land, by sea, and by air

> *"Now, as wonderful as it would be to be able to create a one-size-fits-all process, that is just never the case. Good adoption practices some in all different shapes and sizes, and it best to always take different approaches."*
> Meredith Williams Range

To maximize the number of attorneys exposed to the newly on-boarded technology, execute with your vendor on a plan that addresses all the ways your attorneys learn. Then rinse and repeat.

The best firm-wide roll-outs often start with identifying and spotlighting champions. As Rich Robbins from Sidley Austin says:

> *"We look for evangelists, champions. A reference from a trusted colleague is gold. So the best scenario is when we have secured enthusiastic support from influencers within the firm."*

With key champions lined up, Williams-Range advises:

> *"Then move[s] to webinars, in-person training, etc. Finally, we attend practice group meetings and make the presentations very practical for the groups."*

Add on vendor-lead office hours, handouts, and gamification to spur usage, and the only element missing is sheer persistence.

Nittel from Allen Matkins suggests that:

> *"You can't take no for an answer. No one is going to understand it the first time. They care about how the technology can save or make money. It's all about being persistent. Talk about it a lot, make sure they know they are not going to be replaced. There have been times when you will be told to leave. Come back tomorrow. After a while, they will give in…"*

Put a different way, but reinforcing the value of persistence in spurring adoption, Lowman observed that:

> *"Like anything else that's new, we have worked to keep getting in front of people to remind them of the opportunity and value of new technology. How many times have you decided to finally act on something after being reminded four or five times?"*

Some attorneys learn from reading, some from listening. Others learn from active discussions. Says Agnihotri:

> *"New technology can be met with mistrust, criticism, and can be considered a threat and not worthy of the time and effort needed to learn it. One-way passive communications can be good reminders; we also focus on engaging the lawyers in discussions so that they are forced to think about how the change helps them."*

Keep it simple – equip your attorneys with the vocabulary to effectively communicate the tool within the firm and to their clients

> *"I don't think it is hard to get attorneys to use technology as long as you frame your message in a way that imparts value to them."* Marlene Gebauer

Legal technology experts agree that focusing on plain English and not newfangled buzzwords will increase the chances that your product will be successfully adopted. Agnihotri concurs that it's wise to "tone down any technical jargon to avoid an artificial barrier to learning. We choose to deliberately cover only the most key features of a new tool in the first wave of adoption; else we would risk the users being overwhelmed and turned off."

In an echo of the "use case over the shiny object" theme, Gebauer notes:

"I think if you can frame how users will benefit their practice and their clients by reducing risk, improving work product, providing more consistency, or perhaps by allowing more collaboration and integration with clients on mutually beneficial solutions, it is a more compelling argument to a practitioner than something they perceive will take work away from them."

Chapter 8:
We're ready to be innovative – now what?

By Chris Austin, director of information governance, Bowman and Brooke

Introduction

"Everyone wants to be innovative, but nobody wants to change." Those words ring true at a mid-sized law firm. We all want the fastest and latest tools and software; however, most people don't want to change and are "stuck in their ways".

Even if change is truly innovative and is in the best interest of the firm, change can be a difficult uphill battle. Mid-sized law firms are filled with experienced attorneys and legal administrators who have built successful careers by following a proven path that has pushed them to the top of their profession. Because the past has proven to be successful for these individuals, your innovative change may face resistance. It will need to go through many stages, so your firm and the people in it can adjust, allowing them to achieve even greater heights.

Mid-sized law firms vary in size and cultures; to quantify the steps to bring about innovative change within your firm is futile. However, there are a few ideas that I have found to work. This chapter focuses on a few of those unconventional ways that have proven to help facilitate change.

Ultimately, innovation comes down to execution. It doesn't matter how innovative or revolutionary a product or service is if you can't get it into the hands of the people who will benefit. But before we jump into the steps, it's important to go over some basic prerequisites.

Prerequisites for innovation

First, you need to know your firm. Know the practice groups, the strategic plan, your major clients, and what direction the firm is going. This is basic knowledge for most leaders, but what is often written in a strategic plan or on a webpage can contradict what is actually happening within the firm. Understanding that there is a difference between how things *should be* and how they *actually are* is vital. Having a deep understanding of the firm can give insight on finding key issues and where innovation fits in.

Second, it's critical to know the people in the firm. At a mid-sized law firm, you have a unique advantage of being relatively small in terms of headcount. This small headcount allows you to know people at a deep level. Understand who they are as people, what makes them tick, what are their dreams, aspirations, complaints, and fears. Know which people will help you and which will resist. You also need to know how individuals are respected within the firm. While you want everyone to benefit from your innovation, not everybody will. You'll need to find allies that hold credibility and are pioneers of innovation. It doesn't matter what position your allies hold, only that others in the firm value and listen to their opinion. Knowing everyone in the firm at a deep level gives you a huge advantage.

Finally, know your problem. Specifically, know the problem that your technology is set to solve. Is your solution solving a true pain point or are you making problems bigger than they appear to be? Often, we're enticed to follow products and ideas that only lower costs. Most people are not motivated by costs or cost savings. How is your innovative technology going to make their lives better? Is the technology fixing a big problem or a minor nuisance? Incremental change and cost savings are good; however, to bring about large, innovative change, your message needs to be clear and concise, and a key part of that message is understanding the problem you're trying to solve.

A deep understanding of your firm, the people and the problem is crucial. Understanding these three variables to the greatest extent possible will make change easier and is essential to carrying out the items below.

Communication

Communication is key in any organization but for mid-sized law firms it can be particularly tricky. There is limited time for everyone. Often executives, directors, and managers are wearing multiple hats and doing multiple jobs, while partners, associates, and paralegals have large billable hour requirements. To put it bluntly, members of a mid-sized firm are extremely busy and only small windows of time exist to capture their time and attention.

With all our advances in technology, a mid-sized firm still relies heavily on verbal and email communication. The trick to overcome the barriers in communication comes down to communicating in a unique way to grab their attention and spark action to promote change.

Email communication

Capture their attention

Most people have a limited attention span and are juggling multiple responsibilities at one time so capturing your audience's attention can be challenging. I have found a few tricks to capture attention with email.

First, individualize the message to a single person or a very small group. Often, I see people create broad email messages for a large group. When large group messages are sent, they're often ignored. Long emails don't inspire or address individual concerns. Readers can quickly assess an email simply by skimming the subject line. Worse yet, busy legal executives will often ignore group emails altogether, assuming subordinates will read the email and let them know if there is a concern.

Group email messages are subject to group think responses. This can be particularly troublesome in the early stages of change when not everyone is up to speed on your ideas. If a "reply all" email is sent in response to your email and objects to your proposal, you'll need to overcome the objection from the person who responded. In addition, you'll also need to overcome that same objection for everybody else on the email chain. This can also fuel unneeded negative objections and questions that will detract from the positive momentum that you're trying to create.

Group email communication does not inspire your audience. People will feel that they are lumped into the masses. You want your reader to feel like they are part of the innovation and a leader in the future of the firm. Group emails will not do this.

While drafting multiple emails is much more work for you, consider the end results. With smaller messages that are tailored to your audience, your message is much more likely to be noticed, read and ultimately adopted.

Simplify the message

As humans, our attention span gets shorter and shorter. Getting to the point, especially in emails, is of the utmost importance. In my own experience, I've found that there's a direct correlation between the length of an email and whether I read it or not. Long drawn out emails that detail every element of a subject routinely go unread or deleted without being looked at it. Busy legal executives simply do not have the time to read all their emails and the longer the email is, the easier it is to skip and dismiss. Get to the point quickly and directly. Be polite but remember small talk is best left to social hours, lunches, and coffee breaks. While this may seem cold or rude, in a mid-sized firm where there are never enough hours in a day, wasting time with pleasantries via email when trying to bring about change to save time or money is counterintuitive.

More than likely, your new innovative product contains many benefits. As tempting as it is to list all the great features, DON'T! Try to stay with the one or two major features that your innovative product does. If you feel compelled to list multiple features, keep it to a bullet-point list. Telling your reader about all the benefits and features in your initial email sabotages your goal – commitment. You rob your reader of exploring and drawing their own conclusions when implementation begins. Furthermore, if you tell your audience everything about the product, they may end up drawing their own conclusions, and those conclusions run the risk of being negative. Email correspondence is not a place where you can easily turn those incorrect conclusions around.

Testimonials

One of my favorite techniques when communicating via email is to use short testimonials from other users who support the initiative. Testimonials from well-respected lawyers and legal administrators help validate the product and get your reader to feel as though they are missing out.

Testimonials help tell the story about innovation through a different lens and voice. This is a subtle way to show the reader that it is not just you (the author of the email) who supports this product, but others do as well. It is another layer validating your innovation.

Testimonials can take shape many ways. Usually during the evaluation stage of a product, you will gather feedback from those who are participating in the evaluation. That feedback can be used to create a list of testimonials. Testimonials can include a detailed account of a feature, or a simple broad testimonial that invokes excitement such as "This is awesome!" Testimonials give color and personality to your email and help validate the innovation.

Email timing

Timing of an email is crucial and can be difficult to determine. Many people will send their well-crafted email immediately after they have finished writing it. This is a normal approach. However, timing can make or break your message. If you send an email on the afternoon at the end of the week, you run the risk of your reader not seeing it for several days. And even if they do read your email on a Friday afternoon, they probably won't remember it come Monday morning. Alternatively, sending an email in the middle of the workday can be just as bad. Mid-sized law firms are bustling with energy throughout the day. There are filing deadlines, depositions, and client meetings happening at breakneck speed. Sending an email during the busiest part of the day will likely go unnoticed.

In my experience, I have found that sending an email early in the morning works best. While not all people operate the same, I find most people arrive at work, grab a cup of coffee and review their email from the previous day or night. If you can get your email in front of your audience prior to the day's demands, you at least have a chance that they will read and hopefully reflect on your message.

Verbal communication

Verbal communication will go much further than email. Verbal communication allows both sides to ask questions and become at ease with the project. If possible, in person verbal communication is best, as opposed to video chat or a phone call. When in person, you can read non-verbal cues much more easily. You can tell if someone is getting excited about the product or if they're distracted. With all the advantages of being face-to-face there are a few additional things to make it even more effective.

Group size

Like email, you want to limit the size of your group during verbal communication. When in person with a small group, you're able to engage people on a personal level. The smaller the number of people in the group, the greater attention you will give to each individual. You can address any concerns they have immediately. You'll also learn about objections people may have and learn how to overcome those objections on the spot. Because you'll have to hold more sessions with smaller groups than a single large group, this will prepare you for what to expect in future conversations.

By listening and communicating with individuals you can invoke empathy. People will feel they are being listened to and are more likely to listen to you. This in turn will provide them with a feeling of involvement and that can help you communicate your message to others.

Storytelling

Storytelling is a great way to bring meaning and context to your innovation. Tell stories of how your idea has already helped similar people. This will give them a feeling of involvement and even may invoke fear that they are missing out. Storytelling can also give credibility to your innovation. It is not just about you, but about others who are already onboard with this new and exciting innovation.

Stories are more likely to be remembered as opposed to statistics or hypotheticals. Most people are likely to relate and understand a story rather than a fact-filled email. A story will give much more meaning to the new innovative technology.

Simplify the message

At a mid-sized firm, it is common to be pulled away to take care of an urgent matter. You never know when your audience might need to quickly shuffle off, therefore your verbal message needs to be simple.

Keeping your message simple does a few things. First, you're assured that you will get the main points out to your audience in the event they get pulled away. Second, by keeping things simple, the audience can build their own conclusions. Having your audience draw their own conclusions is much more powerful for long-term commitment than you trying to convince them. Finally, by keeping your message simple, this may invoke your audience to want more information about the technology. You may have just piqued their curiosity enough to get them to start chasing you, instead of you trying to convince them.

Excite the audience

Above all, excite the audience. It's very important to make sure that you're excited to talk to individuals about your innovative product. Be excited, smile and laugh. Be a good listener and meet any objections head on. Excitement and enthusiasm are contagious. If people see you're excited, they will naturally be excited too. After all, if you're not excited about the product, you can't expect your audience to be.

Timing

Access to the system

In change management, one consideration is how and when to roll-out the technology. Organizations will typically rip and replace technology. They focus on an official launch date and when they turn on the new system they expect fanfare and celebration. Often the opposite happens; they experience confusion, questions, downtime, and general dissatisfaction over the new technology. This can be avoided by staging the roll-out in small increments. Of course, there are times when this is not possible due to the size, scope, and impact of the project, but if possible try to roll-out in stages.

When using a staged approach to roll-out software, try granting access to the system immediately after training. This has many advantages:

- If training is a success, users will want to use the technology immediately. Waiting to give access in a distant future only invites forgetfulness and urgency is lost;
- Immediate access gives users the ability to "test" the technology to their own experience. They can come to their own conclusions outside of the training environment;
- Through their own exploration, users will come up with additional questions. Later, when you follow up, this will give you an opportunity to engage each person directly; and
- If access is given prior to training, you run the risk of people trying it, not understanding fully the operations, and then getting frustrated. At that point, chances are that you've lost them as a credible user and they will more than likely skip the scheduled training.

Follow up

After training you should give yourself time to follow up. Go office by office, desk by desk, to make sure all users can log in and get comfortable with the new system. As difficult as it may be, try and get to every person. Following up individually gives you a chance to reinforce principles that were introduced in training. It is important to the users to do the pointing, clicking, and general operations of the technology. This will help users reinforce operations of the technology through their own actions.

Focus on small groups

As with email and verbal communication, rolling out the software should focus on small groups. Leveraging what you know about the firm and people, you can assess when a good time would be to roll-out your technology. This is crucial because mid-sized firms are often bombarded with constant obligations. Offices and case teams may be getting ready for a large trial, holiday event, or key individuals could be away on vacation. If you focus on rolling the technology out to small groups you can get a subset of people completed while others are away or busy.

Leverage the client

When I started working in law firms I heard an expression that has stuck with me. "*This place is about outcomes.*" Serving the client is the goal of a mid-sized firm. Using the client as leverage to propel your technology can be very helpful. Ask yourself, will this technology help with favorable outcomes for the client? Will both the client and the firm mutually benefit in efficiencies because of this innovation? Meaningful innovation will likely impact the client in some fashion.

Sometimes the client will suggest using a new innovative piece of software. This can be particularly powerful with partners and the entire case team. When the firm knows the client is interested in the technology, buy-in and acquiring technology usually becomes much easier.

Clients are becoming more interested in how a law firm works. They want to make sure they're getting the best legal representation at the lowest cost. When a client is interested in innovation, you should be interested too.

Attitude

Champion building

In change management, we typically look for "executive champions", which are those individuals who are in a position of authority to help build momentum. Instead of trying to find and then convince an executive to carry your message, I advocate for a concept of "champion building". Champion building is trying to find well respected people (regardless of position) who will use and love your new innovative product. Once you find these people, you must take great care and responsibility to empower and promote their words and their experiences. Let your champions tell their story to their own network. They will be able to reach many more people than you will alone.

Enthusiasm

Above all is enthusiasm. If you are not enthusiastic about your new innovative product, then you can't expect others to be. Every time you see someone who may benefit, you need to be excited, engaging, and enthusiastic. Approach them as if this innovative technology were the best thing you could do for them.

Conclusion

Working at a mid-sized firm is tough. Attorneys and legal professionals are extremely busy and under extraordinary pressure. Law firm operations are changing rapidly, and innovative people and software will play a crucial role in the future. Bringing meaningful innovative change is quite possibly the most important job you have. The future of your firm and the legal profession depends on it.

Chapter 9:
"Access to the Bar for all", not the few

By Charlotte Ogilvie, marketing and communications executive, Garden Court Chambers

> *"I wear a scarf, I am a short, brown girl. I don't (yet) wear a wig. I have felt out of place in court. I often walk into courtrooms and everyone is an older white man wearing a wig. It used to be intimidating, but I'm getting used to it. Through 'Access to the Bar for All' I can see that I am welcome here and that I am supported."*
>
> Nazia Islam, former sixth form pupil from Oaklands School, Tower Hamlets, London

Race, gender, or socio-economic background should not act as barriers to inclusion; yet today women, people from Black Asian and Minority Ethnic (BAME), and low socio-economic backgrounds remain under-represented at the Bar. In 2018 in the UK, women accounted for 37.4 percent of barristers, and only 15.8 percent of QCs (Queen's Counsel) – a designation given to eminent lawyers who have proven excellence in advocacy.[1] Only 13 percent of barristers are from BAME backgrounds, and only 7.8 percent of those were QCs in 2018. At this rate, it will take 50 years before women comprise half of all QCs and 100 years for the percentage of BAME "silks" – a colloquialism for a member of Queen's Counsel – to mirror the general population. In addition to this, the Bar Standards Board (BSB) has reported that a "disproportionately high percentage of the Bar primarily attended an independent secondary school".[2] This is unacceptable.

In order for the Bar, and the legal sector more widely, to remain both credible and relevant it must go far beyond just recognizing its own lack of diversity, though that is *of course* a necessary step. When we talk about increasing diversity, we must steer well clear of the narrative around a "dilution of standards" – an idea fueled by prejudice, whether conscious or unconscious. The current underrepresentation of women, people from BAME, and low-socio economic backgrounds *clearly* does not derive from any shortage of talent. Rather, the legal profession as we know it does not select from everyone, but from the few, and often those who are the easiest to reach.

It is not in our interest for the Bar to be dominated by people from one background alone. A diversity of experiences and outlooks are needed, and people from underrepresented groups must be shown that the legal sector wants to actively encourage and support them. If anything, people who have faced hardship tend to be more driven, committed, and dedicated than their more privileged counterparts. There are still so many groups that the Bar hasn't warmed up to yet, where raw materials are left untapped and undiscovered from a lack of proactive pursuit. This is changing, and must continue to do so.

In 2017, in an effort to redress this imbalance and accelerate the rate of progress, Garden Court Chambers, which has just under 200 barristers, set up "Access to the Bar for All", a long-term mentoring scheme that encourages students from minority and disadvantaged groups to consider a career as a barrister. The scheme is now entering its third year, and it is constantly evolving.

Khadeza Ali, one of six young women in our first cohort, who is now in her second year of History and English at Queen Mary University of London, says, "The reality is the Bar is not anywhere near as diverse as it should be". Exposure, she believes, both *for* young people from diverse backgrounds, and *to* them, is vital to making change. "If someone different is right in front of you, naturally your mind is going to start thinking about them," she says. "My differences are very obvious… I am of a different race. I am of a different religion. I am a woman. And I am covered." Ali explains the significance of the scheme pushing the profession to consider people "like her". "When people see me they are forced to think how to make inclusion happen."

Nazia Islam, another mentee on the scheme, now in her second year studying English Literature at the University of Cambridge, says that she believes that diversity schemes such as "Access to the Bar for All" are necessary to encourage and support people from all sections of society, and especially those who aren't always able to enter the legal profession without them. Islam maintains that they will not only benefit the individuals taking part, but the legal profession and justice system more widely. She says, "We need to have more women representing women on women's issues, and more practitioners from diverse backgrounds representing the diverse communities that make up our country".

What sparked the scheme?

In November 2016, Garden Court Chambers won an award for public and administrative law. Leslie Thomas QC – chair and joint head of Garden Court Chambers, who attended the awards ceremony – reported seeing less than a handful of black faces in a room of almost 300 people. That same month, Garden Court held an open day for potential pupils and it became apparent that the majority of those from certain socio-economic backgrounds had no experience in chambers, no contacts, and no support to remedy this.

Mia Hakl-Law, our director of Operations and HR, and Connor Johnston, one of our barristers, respectively decided that, in order to address the under-representation of women, ethnic minorities, and people from low socio-economic backgrounds, young people needed to be approached before they decided the legal profession was not for them. They felt that a positive impact could be had if secondary school students had access to mentors when they were 16, before their A-levels (pre-university exams in the UK), that would offer them a helping hand over a long period of time.

Setting up the scheme

Upon realizing that for change to happen we would have to do it ourselves, Mia put forward a proposal at Garden Court Chambers' AGM in January 2017, which was voted through unanimously. The proposed scheme was for small-scale, full support for two students each from three schools in some of the most economically deprived areas of London – Tower Hamlets, Southwark, and Greenwich. At least one of the two young people selected from each school had to be a girl, and at least one had to come from a BAME background. All participants had to be in receipt of free school meals, be the first generation in their family to go to university, and live in an area that is in the top 10 percent of the Multiple Index of Deprivation. The participants were selected through a formal recruitment process run by Chambers.

The successful candidates were then offered mentoring from a barrister for five years, three weeks of paid work experience per year, and the opportunity to be awarded a £7,000 scholarship to assist with living expenses for each year of university if they went on to study a law degree at undergraduate level.

After the scheme was voted in, Mia sent out a message asking for six tenants to commit to volunteering as mentors over a five-year period. Twenty barristers volunteered within 30 minutes.

"I thought it was a fantastic idea to have a scheme that was very concentrated on a handful of mentees, but long term that would give very concrete practical and financial support to young people from specific backgrounds," says Di Middleton QC, barrister at Garden Court Chambers, who was previously a mentor through the scheme. She continues:

> *"It's very special to be able to make such a substantial difference to one person's life. This is not just a leg-up in a financial year for an organization. It is a massively influential scheme with tangible benefits for the participants in their actual development and in their introduction to adulthood... One of the things I like about the scheme is the fact that we choose carefully where the mentees come from and let class and economic background feature in it – not just more obvious inequalities like ethnicity or gender."*

Funding the scheme

The cost is spread across all members of Chambers over a five-year period. Since its inception, Garden Court Chambers has operated the Special Fund, a unique source of funding within the legal profession. Every member of Chambers, of which we have around 200, contributes financially to the Special Fund through a percentage of their yearly earnings. It primarily makes donations to small, progressive, cutting-edge organizations doing legal, campaigning, or charitable work in defense of civil liberties and/or access to social justice. All funds for "Access to the Bar for All" come from this resource. All members of Chambers are invested both financially, and on a deeper level that is tangible through the positive interactions between tenants and mentees.

The application process

When it was agreed that the scheme was going ahead, it was decided that three schools should be chosen. Mia contacted schools which, in previous years, had asked Garden Court to take students for work experience; she also contacted the National Union of Teachers, seeking recommendations of which areas in London to aim for in terms of deprivation levels. She then pitched the scheme to a number of schools, who responded positively to her initial call. The final three were then selected based on the levels of interest and proactivity from the heads of sixth form, including how successful they had been in getting students interested and involved in the introduction sessions that she had delivered.

A group of barristers in Chambers devised an application form that was sent to schools for interested students to fill in. They had to fulfil the criteria mentioned above, but also respond to questions about their motivation and current affairs.

The application forms were then assessed, and the most promising candidates were invited to Chambers to attend a formal panel interview. For most of the young people who made it to the interview stage, it was a novel experience.

Joey Liu, who is now a second year History student at the University of Exeter, joined the scheme as a sixth form pupil at Walworth Academy, Southwark. She reflects on her experience of the interview process:

> *"It was the scariest thing... The questions were unexpected. It sounded daunting beforehand, but when it came around, the barristers were really friendly. They just wanted to get to know us and find out if we were the best candidates for the scheme. It was actually quite therapeutic just to have someone asking me questions and making me reflect on why I really want to do this."*

The scheme

Mentoring

All participants are paired with a barrister who will be their mentor for the duration of the scheme. Mentors provide participants with someone to interact with on a regular basis outside of their normal spheres. Liu says:

> *"It's good to have someone to talk to – not your parent, not your teacher, not your friend, but someone outside of it all who doesn't know you, but you get to tell them things, learn from them, exchange ideas, and it's just between you."*

All mentors and mentees keep in contact by phone and email, and most pairs meet face-to-face roughly every two months. Islam's mentor is Ann Osborne, a family barrister at Garden Court.

> *"Ann and I meet up. We message each other... We talk things over quite often, and I keep her posted on how I'm getting on at university. It's good to have someone outside of my loop to discuss things with and she often gives me new perspectives that I might not otherwise have considered."*

"We must put our money where our mouth is, and the scheme offers meaningful financial support," says Middleton. "Initially the money seemed like a really important benefit. Yes, it's part of it, but it's so much more than a financial assistance scheme."

She believes that what has even greater weight and makes "Access to the Bar for All" so unique is the long-term relationship and the exposure that comes with it. There is a "constant channel" between the mentee and their mentor, Chambers, and the Bar more widely. Giving someone the opportunity to "knock about" in Chambers, to meet barristers, attend social functions, go into court, and to have someone on the end of a phone or an email who is invested in them is invaluable. Says Middleton QC:

> *"Being in the environment and growing comfortable with it is so much part of this scheme. It's amazing to see someone becoming less and less self-conscious, and being able to really properly give hands-on help. I've seen Joey develop into someone gleaming with confidence."*

In the first year of the scheme, Liu worked with her previous mentor, Middleton QC, on her application for university, stating that the constructive criticism offered, along with Middleton QC's ability to ask the right questions, was important in helping form a personal statement that Liu said really "sounded like me". Based on her application she was given conditional offers to study law at the University of Exeter – where she now studies History – or the University of Warwick, both prestigious universities in the UK. In her personal statement, after a discussion with Middleton QC, Liu wrote about the differences between court proceedings in immigration tribunals and criminal law, which made an impression on her.

> *"Tribunals are held in rooms like classrooms, but criminal courts are huge, old-fashioned, and much more what you might expect. I noticed that there's such a massive difference and wondered if that represented the importance attributed to immigrants in this country. It's almost as if they're not given enough attention, or their cases aren't valued as much. It's not just the physical scenery though, but also the Home Office. I could really feel the hostile environment."*

Connor Johnston, before becoming Liu's mentor in the second year of the scheme, was a "satellite mentor". At that point he had not yet been assigned a mentee, and instead offered support with more ad hoc mentoring duties such as providing mock interviews for university. Islam benefited from this support and had a trial run before her interview to study English Literature at Cambridge, where she is now in her second year.

> *"It was very tailored... It's different to being interviewed by your teachers who you know almost too well. The reality is that when you do go to the interview you don't know the people sitting in front of you. Having a fresh face asking me questions I wouldn't expect was so helpful. Afterwards, he also gave me feedback on what I needed to improve and praise for the things that I was already doing well. I realized that an interview doesn't have to be stressful, or tense. Interviewers are not trying to trick you – they are trying to bring out the best in you."*

Johnston, reflecting on the experience, said:

> *"She didn't need much coaching. The most useful thing I could do was give her validation. She hasn't had any awards to show her she's brilliant, but she has all of the raw materials she needs – all she was lacking was a bit of reassurance that she was good enough."*

Liu says, "I know I want to get into law", while recognizing that it's not going to be easy. She has discussed at length how she will get there with her mentor, Johnston, who she says has given her a valuable lesson in perspective.

> *"Connor has showed me that there is no rush. I think having another career first would be a good option for me, and then – when I'm a bit more well-rounded and knowledgeable – I can apply to the Bar."*

Liu says that she feels a lot of pressure, and that on top of her questioning herself, other people – sometimes those who don't even know her – do the same. Outlining some of the barriers she faces, along with the other mentees, she says:

> *"It's the sexism. The racism. The expense... On top of that, I'm really young."*

Undertaking a career in law is a huge investment, of time and money, and knowing that there is no "right" way to go about it is really reassuring.

Ali, similarly, has benefitted from this perspective.

> *"I think you have to grow into yourself. You have to know what you want and don't want. What you can and can't do. I never want to lose touch with myself."*

She says that she finds it really helpful to have her mentor, Jo Cecil, to bounce ideas off and to help take the pressure off a bit.

"My route to the Bar may not be very conventional. I think it's important to remember that it isn't a race. If anything, if I rush I'm not going to come to the profession with the right experience. There is no cap on time and no one is saying 'if you're not here by [a certain age], you're out'... Jo reminds me to take it one step at a time. One thing that makes me anxious is that I'm a massive planner. I want to know my ten-year plan now. But she [Jo] reassures me that perhaps a ten year vision rather than plan might be better for me. That I'll still get there if I take it slowly. That really helps. She's great."

Ali also praises the long-term nature of the scheme. She says that regularly going into court over a number of years is continuing to push her to grow in confidence in a setting that she initially found "uncomfortable" and "daunting".

"I'm often the only person who looks like me in the [court] room," she says. "People in the public gallery often wonder who I am... [Going into court] for the third summer now, doing it over and over again, has helped me get past the self-consciousness and discomfort."

Over time, she says, she has learned to be more sure and confident of her own more "obvious" differences.

"I am of a BAME background. I am a Muslim. I am a woman. I am hijabi... Not a lot of people who don't necessarily look or speak in the 'conventional' way are lucky enough to have [this] opportunity to go into court, again and again, until they learn to become comfortable with it."

Work experience

"There is no substitute for a working knowledge of what a job actually entails," says Mike Higgins, head of sixth form at Walworth Academy. "It's motivating and they are excited by that. They are excited by the real job."

Each participant follows three weeks of paid work experience for the duration of the scheme. This is flexible and varies depending on their interests. Liu gained experience of cases regarding black markets, the use of weapons, murder, family disputes, and immigration, stating that the effort made by the barristers to really get her involved in trials has "given [her] a real insight into how things actually work". Tomi Adagunodo

– a previous pupil at Walworth Academy, Southwark – and Islam, who attended Oaklands School, also saw a wide spread of different proceedings during their work experience. Hannah Dalton, former head of sixth form at Oaklands School, emphasizes:

> *"Lots of law firms and chambers offer work shadowing, work placements or e-mentoring, but for students like ours being dropped into a company for one week is not going to change their mindset or perspective in any long-term or meaningful way."*

Islam comments that being so close to cases has helped her make a view of the law itself, and not just the legal profession, and develop a deeper understanding of the mechanics of the system:

> *"It's so useful working with people who are instructed in cases every day – being able to witness them, react to them, be curious and ask anything you want, to get answers to your questions straightaway and discuss them with someone who is so knowledgeable... That's something that I haven't been able to find anywhere else."*

During the work experience, participants also spend time with a range of barristers who are not their mentors. This is a chance for them to grow their contacts and be exposed to a broader group of practitioners working on different areas of law. Liu says of this aspect:

> *"I feel that this program has enabled me to build up my network... Being part of this has helped me grow in confidence and I find it so much easier to communicate with people now... I've learned how to be professional... and feel like I've become an adult as part of the process."*

Similarly, Adagunodo says:

> *"Since starting at Garden Court my communication skills have improved and I know how to target my speech and pitch things at the right level. I'm more adaptable now, more confident and more engaged with current affairs."*

As "Access to the Bar for All" is a new scheme, year-on-year, it is evolving. This year we introduced the opportunity for mentees to work as (paid) administrative staff at Garden Court for three months over the summer, to expand their knowledge of the workings of Chambers "behind the scenes".

Liu says:

> *"Working in chambers, as part of the staff behind closed doors, is interesting and it has helped me to narrow down which barristers I want to work with and shadow in court. At the moment I'm in the reprographics room. I meet so many barristers all the time who work on so many different areas of law. Quite often [when they come down to pick up their printing] we have a chat about what they're working on. They're usually really friendly, and I'm learning a lot about them."*

In addition to the personal connections, Liu says that she appreciates that doing this role has "really helped [her] see the break-down of Chambers and how it works on a day-to-day basis."

Wider exposure

"On my first day of work experience, I went to Luton Crown Court. I was the only girl there and the only black person. It's quite shocking to see the lack of ethnic minority practitioners at the Bar. It's usually the ethnic minorities who are the defendants and that's really sad," says Adagunodo.

However, being part of the scheme, she has got to know several women from ethnic minority backgrounds working in the law.

> *"I remember shadowing Ann Osborne. She's black. I could identify with her. It was inspirational to meet someone like me in a job like this, and a profession like this. I think it's important to be able to see people who look like you, who sound like you, and who come from the same background."*

Islam commented on the position of women within the profession and suggests that it is not women themselves but the structure of the legal profession that doesn't always create the kind of space that they need.

"It's disheartening, but it makes me more determined," she says.

> *"I love that this scheme is aimed at girls – it's been amazing being around such intelligent women, both my peers and my superiors. I just feed off them. It's great to have such impressive role models – especially women from similar backgrounds to me – and I've met quite a few already. Every time I see one particular barrister at Garden Court Chambers I'm just so inspired. She is exactly what I picture when I think of a successful, confident woman: the way she is in court, how she talks to people – that's what I want to be like. I want to be just as strong."*

Why we need access to the Bar for *all*, not just a select few

Liu talks about her experience of moving from South East London to study at the University of Exeter. She said it was a "massive culture shock" and that she was taken aback, coming from multicultural London to a much more homogenous setting where her ethnic background was suddenly much more noticeable, as well as her socio-economic background. She said that initially she was intimidated by her course mates who "talk like they know the textbook like the back of their hand" and that sometimes she was made to feel like an outsider. However, despite the clear advantages her middle-class counterparts might have in terms of finance and confidence, Liu says through her involvement in "Access to the Bar" she is in a "good position".

> *"I know a few barristers. I get along with them. It's not like I just have their numbers [through a family friend], but I work with them, I talk to them on a regular basis and I'm learning from them all the time."*

Liu also says that whenever she talks about the scheme people always respond with great interest.

> *"Not only has the scheme opened up doors for me into the law, but it gives me something to talk about at university. I feel that it, fairly or unfairly, gives me a kind of credibility and people start treating me with more respect."*

Though she appreciates having this "point of interest", and the social credits this endows upon her, she asks, "Is it just through this scheme that I have proved myself to [them]?"

Do class-divisions, in particular, present themselves as a hurdle that must be "jumped" and subsequently "left behind"? Should access to the Bar, and acceptance within it, require people from diverse backgrounds to overcome their differences, by minimizing them as much as possible? Is diversity so undervalued that the ultimate goal is homogeneity? Arguably, the Bar should be apologetic for not embracing difference enough, rather than individuals from underrepresented groups apologizing for who they are, but more than anything, where they come from. Ali, reflecting on the current situation, says:

> *"If you want to have good lawyers, and you want to have justice, then naturally you have to have a wide range of people who are allowed to, and actively encouraged to, access the Bar."*

If there is a situation where people from underrepresented groups feel unwelcome, or like they don't have a way in, she says:

> *"The same system will be perpetuated. Allowing young people from BAME and working-class backgrounds, and/or women to come in and experience [the Bar] and see that the inside is a place that they need to aspire to be in so that they can make change is vital. You can't sit on the outside and change it. You have to understand it fully and be part of it to have an impact."*

Ali also points out that the "Access to the Bar" scheme is not just of huge benefit to the young people who are being supported, but that recruiting diverse talent brings a new perspective and pushes people, especially those who have been practicing for a while, to think in a different way.

The reality is, quite often, diversity schemes are run by people who are not necessarily in tune with what it is like to be young *now*, or to be at the receiving end of law and legislation in their communities and their own lives. Ali gives the example of cases where having a more diverse Bar would be an advantage, and would save time and money. She shares that she has shadowed a number of cases where defendants giving evidence were being asked to "break-down and clarify what each word they were saying meant" when using non-traditional English, especially in online communications, for example through messaging applications such as WhatsApp.

> *"I knew that the jury could understand the words, and the 'translations' were largely for the lawyers. The lack of understanding of youth language and young culture is a real problem at the moment and it can dictate the result of certain cases, especially relating to those of a certain demographic. Sometimes it feels like the lawyers make out like a word is more meaningful than it is. It's frustrating that this gap in knowledge is dictating the way the law is working."*

How other chambers or firms can help widen the scheme

"For what you're able to achieve and the help you're able to give the participants, the financial impact on Chambers is really minimal," says Middleton QC. Even in a Chambers the size of Garden Court, the cost of supporting six mentees over the duration of the scheme is manageable, and places no financial burden on members as they are paying the same into the Special Fund as they were before the scheme was set up in 2017.

"It's such a substantial scheme and it doesn't need to take away from anything you might be doing already. It's possible for small chambers to take on something similar to make a difference to individuals' lives. If every chambers took on even one young person and carried them through university – whether through mentoring, work experience, or financial assistance – imagine how many people could be helped and the impact that it would have."

It could easily be a daunting prospect for a set of chambers or a firm to start up their own initiatives without any guidance. However, we hope that this chapter will go some way towards assisting others on setting up something similar to promote diversity, and effect wider change within the legal sector.

Says Liu:

"The program is a huge stepping stone for people interested in law," "and it should definitely be taken on by more chambers and firms. There are so many people who want to succeed, but there aren't always these opportunities for them to grab onto. I think that the only way we can make the legal sector more balanced is by actively seeking out BAME students."

One of the benefits of "Access to the Bar for All" is that it is small and manageable, making it affordable and achievable, not just for large organizations. The main hinge upon which the scheme turns is the fact that all lawyers involved as mentors are volunteers, which means that a firm's costs are not massively increased by their engagement. "There is no financial incentive for them," Liu explains, "but they should be motivated to educate younger people from different backgrounds who don't necessarily have a whole system behind them. Sometimes young people like that – like me – need that extra support."

Dalton, Oaklands School, said:

"There are very few schemes, currently, which recognize the many barriers faced by young people when applying for the Bar, such as being closed out by well-connected, fee-paying contemporaries and the overwhelming costs of university and the Bar course. Garden Court Chambers' scheme is so good because it recognizes that one-week shadowing schemes, common across the legal field, have little impact on increasing diversity at the Bar as they don't address the issues faced by young people from underprivileged backgrounds. The longer view taken by this scheme is crucial because the barristers provide support to students beyond the sixth form

as they make choices at university, where typically there is little specialized guidance available."

There is an overrepresentation at the Bar of those who attended fee-paying schools, and barristers are more likely than not to have at least one parent who went to university. We hope that many other chambers and law firms will follow suit and will set up their own long-term schemes to address the lack of diversity at the Bar and tap into the rich vein of talent available from underrepresented groups, who have so much to gain by being welcomed and supported by the legal profession, but also *so much to offer.*

Mia Hakl-Law, director of HR and Operations at Chambers, is happy to be contacted in relation to the scheme and offer guidance, provide further information or answer any in-depth questions.

Garden Court is thrilled and honored to have won the Chambers Diversity Initiative of the Year at the UK Diversity Legal Awards in November 2017 for our long-term mentoring scheme.

Reference

1. www.barstandardsboard.org.uk/media/1975681/diversity_at_the_bar_2018.pdf
2. *Ibid.*

Chapter 10:
Strategic thinking for mid-sized law firms

By John Sterling, chief marketing officer, Sterne Kessler Goldstein & Fox

This chapter addresses the challenges associated with thinking and managing strategically in the current legal marketplace. Is the only strategy for mid-sized firms to merge and grow ("grow or die")? Or, are there other ways to think strategically about market position and capture competitive advantages in ways that are largely independent of size?

We'll tackle these questions from a couple of perspectives. First, we'll discuss fundamental elements of strategic thinking – applicable to virtually any organization, but particularly relevant for mid-size firms. Second, we'll look at strategic considerations that should be relevant to an overwhelming majority of mid-sized firms (i.e., considerations specific to the circumstances most mid-sized firms face today). Finally, we'll conclude with an overview of perhaps the most valuable analytical tool available to mid-sized firms vis-à-vis settling on strategic priorities.

Fundamental elements of strategic thinking for mid-sized law firms

The demise of the mid-sized firm has been predicted for 30 years (essentially since Steve Brill launched *The American Lawyer* and the AmLaw100 listings). The enduring success of many mid-sized firms suggests merger-fueled growth is certainly not the only strategy, but choosing a winning strategy really depends on what your firm aspires to become. Agreeing on a vision and purpose (i.e., who are we and what we want to become) is a precursor to setting a winning strategy. That can mean dedicating the firm to substantial growth, or it can mean adopting a direction that is entirely different (and differentiating).

Developing and building support for a strategic direction for a law firm is a chapter-length topic in itself, so for purposes of this chapter, let's begin with the assumption that there is widespread agreement among the partners regarding a compelling direction (whatever it might be). Further, let's assume that direction is something other than "grow dramatically via merger". In that case, there are a number of things a firm can (in fact should) do to translate that agreed upon strategic direction into a winning strategy.

Focus on a few things that can create a competitive advantage

Competitive advantage for most organizations emerges from being focused. That means saying "yes" to relatively few things, and setting other alternatives to the side. But, how does a firm decide what those "few things" are? Two steps can help to provide clarity on what those focal points might be. First, honestly assess what the firm is truly great at doing. Competitive advantage is built on strengths that can become the epicenter of genuine excellence for the entire firm. Second, get external validation that being great at those things is meaningful in the marketplace. Said simply, focus on a handful of things you are great at (or can become great at) that also have meaning in the market.

A basic SWOT assessment (strengths, weaknesses, opportunities, and threats) can highlight your areas of strength (actual and latent). If your firm is not good at looking objectively at itself, a good consultant can help.

External validation can and should come from clients. A firm's best clients want it to succeed into the future – they almost certainly consider the firm's partners to be among their most trusted advisers. So, ask clients served by many practice areas what the firm is good at and what it can do better. It will inform the firm's strategy and improve client relationships to boot. It is amazing how few firms gather genuine, strategic input from clients in any systematic way.

Think strategically

What does that mean, to think strategically? Well, at a minimum, think about competitive advantage (core strengths the firm might focus its energies on) through three lenses:

- *Scale* – Consider whether the firm enjoys size or scale advantages over competitors in some way. In many markets mid-sized firms are the largest (or nearly the largest) firm in their "home" city. If that is the case for your firm, consider strategies that can leverage that local scale advantage (e.g., visibility, civic involvement, thought leadership, referral relationships with similarly positioned banks/accountancies etc.). For mid-sized firms in larger cities that must compete with large national/global firms, it is helpful to understand the scale advantages of Big Law competitors as well. Large firms do have deeper pockets (or at least more equity partner pockets) over which to spread marketing, technology, and other shared costs. In short, understand scale advantages from both perspectives – those your firm may enjoy, as well as the advantages larger competitors may have over your firm;

- *Defensive positioning* – Identify factors that may help the firm to defend its market position against competitors (even much larger, better financed competitors). It may be the firm and its partners' knowledge of the local courts and judges; its reputation and brand may have deep roots in the community; it may have very deep and broad relationships with the best companies in the area. Consider how the firm can capitalize on and solidify those defensive advantages; and
- *The indirect approach* – Finally, and potentially most powerfully, consider opportunities to take an indirect approach. Occupy the unoccupied market positions and be willing to do things differently from competitors. This is especially critical if other firms in the market enjoy scale advantages over your own firm. Precedent is a horrible source of strategy – don't do what others are doing, do things no one else is doing. Being different can play out in many ways – from where you recruit your people, to the tools and processes they use to serve clients, to the clients and industries the firm pursues with purpose.

Implement – do what you say you are going to do

Two factors drive success more than any others – having a clear sense of direction (i.e., vision, purpose, shared values), and implementing effectively on priorities. I and others have written extensively on strategy implementation.[1] Ultimately, successful implementation in a mid-sized law firm involves:

- Cascading strategy implementation throughout the organization – from firm level initiatives, to practice level activities, to a vital and meaningful role in implementation for all of the firm's people (partners, associates, and staff);
- Measuring and monitoring implementation and the results it is producing – reinvesting in and celebrating the things that are working; and
- Adjusting as implementation unfolds – abandoning or recalibrating initiatives that are clearly not producing expected results and

responding to new market challenges and opportunities as they arise.

Being mid-sized is not equivalent to being diagnosed with a fatal disease. You are free to reject the label and seek to grow – others have done so with remarkable success. But, you can also adopt other winning strategies by focusing on a few sources of competitive advantage, thinking strategically, and implementing with discipline.

Strategy considerations specific to (most) mid-sized firms

According to the most recent *National Law Journal* count, there are over 250 law firms based in the US with between 100 and 500 attorneys. Add to that total another 100 or more firms slightly smaller than 100 attorneys (or that do not report numbers to the NLJ). While those totals do include a handful of large specialty boutiques (e.g., IP firms, labor and employment firms, etc.), most mid-sized firms share some common characteristics.

- Successful mid-size firms tend to be general service, business law firms (although not "full service" – that is unattainable even at 2,500+ lawyers);
- A large number (perhaps a majority) of mid-sized firm's clients are middle market companies – and that means that legal costs are essentially paid out of the owner and/or CEO's pocket;
- Successful mid-sized firms have people and/or practices that are the absolute best in the local/regional market in their areas of expertise; and
- They have at some point (perhaps frequently) been approached by another law firm (probably a larger law firm) interested in merging.

There are important strategic implications associated with each of these traits, each suggesting potential sources of competitive advantage and vulnerabilities to competitive disadvantages. Some generic strategic thinking can be applied to these common attributes.

General service, business firm

As a diversified law firm, a "general business firm" has an opportunity to build deep, multi-practice, multi-partner client relationships.

Potential advantage: Partners at mid-sized firms have a strong personal familiarity with (most of) their partners. That should provide an advantage relative to introducing one another to clients as new needs arise (assuming partners have confidence in one another).

Potential disadvantage: Every firm has practice capability gaps and those gaps can be pretty large in a mid-sized firm (even in the strongest). When competing against Big Law, mid-sized firms need to avoid competing on the basis of scale or breadth. Further, mid-sized firms need trustworthy colleagues to whom they can refer work the firm does not do (e.g., a go-to referral point for IP matters or other areas of practice not covered by the firm).

Middle market clientele

Serving middle market companies has preconditioned many partners at mid-sized firms to be value conscious. The legal market has been moving decisively toward reduced costs and value, particularly since the great recession. Some mid-sized firms have benefited from that trend.

Potential advantage: Generally speaking, rates are lower in mid-sized firms. In addition, many mid-sized firms are predisposed (temperamentally and practically) to staff matters with lean teams.

Potential disadvantage: Big Law firms are making substantial investments in knowledge management, project management, artificial intelligence, data science, and financial management. Those investments have the potential to close rate and efficiency advantages currently enjoyed by mid-sized firms. In addition, large firms have deep enough pockets to price matters aggressively to get in the door – it isn't sustainable for a Big Law firm, but it is a real threat to competing mid-sized firms.

Market leading practices/practitioners

Strong mid-sized firms are often the best choice in their local or regional market for a number of legal issues. Yet, they often are not the largest or most visible firm in their own market.

Potential advantage: Marketing and business development that supports market leading practices generally has the best return on investment. That includes both investments intended to attract new clients and those intended to expand existing relationships across practice areas. The key is being willing to make those investments. The final section of this chapter provides an overview of an analytical approach that can help a firm make critical decisions regarding where to focus those investments.

Potential disadvantage: Essentially, two can play that game (i.e., Big Law competitors will be pushing their own strengths forward in the marketplace) – and larger law firms have larger marketing and business development budgets. In addition, that Big Law competitor may have a great option for the client sitting in an office 2,000 miles away (geography often isn't a barrier for work these days).

Merger inquiries

Critically, you need to know what your firm's general disposition is vis-à-vis merger. Even if it is quickly dismissed by the partners, it is important to have that conversation from time to time at the executive committee or board levels, as well as with the broader partnership.

Beyond that, as a general rule of thumb, mid-sized firm managing partners should accept invitations to lunch from an out-of-town (merger seeking) peer. At worst, you will learn a bit about a firm that is obviously interested in competing for clients and people in your market. And you will gain insights into what other people value in your market and in your firm.

It is worth noting that, while much of this chapter has focused on strategic options and principles that don't involve merger-fueled growth, that is not an entirely irrational strategic direction to adopt. Firms have embraced that direction and some have realized their aspirations beyond perhaps even their own visions. For instance:

- At the time Elliot Portnoy became chairman of the firm in 2007, Sonnenschein, Nath & Rosenthal was a 600-lawyer "Chicago-based law firm". Through a series of mergers, acquisitions, and other growth driven combinations, Dentons has grown to become the world's largest law firm with roughly 10,000 lawyers in 175+ offices across nearly 80 countries.
- Similarly, at the time of their merger in 1999, Piper Marbury was a 400-lawyer "Baltimore law firm" with most of its lawyers located outside money centers, and Rudnick & Wolfe was a 350-lawyer "Chicago real estate powerhouse" with no New York presence at all. DLA Piper is now the world's third largest law firm, with over 3,700 lawyers in 95 cities worldwide.

There are plenty of less dramatic examples of firms growing via merger, improving their financial performance, attracting terrific clients, and expanding their geographic reach. "Moving up market" (as some like to term the strategy) is certainly not impossible. But, as noted above, it is certainly not the only option available to the hundreds of mid-sized firms operating in the marketplace today.

Portfolio analysis – a rational approach to allocating scarce resources

As noted above, nearly all mid-sized firms have some practices and practitioners who have achieved a leading position in the local or regional market. Further, most mid-sized firms have a diversified, general practice service offering. One key strategic decision for general practice firms (mid-sized and larger) is how to allocate scarce resources among those practices – and how to do it in a way that builds competitive advantage in the marketplace. Portfolio analysis and portfolio management provide a set of tools well designed to address these organizationally complex decisions.

Practice groups (generally including industry groups) are in most respects like a strategic business unit in a diversified corporation. They offer distinct services, have unique underlying "production" or operational capabilities, face identifiable competitors, and compete in markets that differ (sometimes dramatically, sometimes subtly) from the markets of other practices. Further, it is entirely possible (in fact, advisable) to measure the financial performance of a practice group – if not on a fully loaded profit and loss basis, then certainly on the basis of contribution to firm profits (e.g., revenues net of direct expenses before the allocation of firm overhead).

Further, given the inherent limitations on resources, it is not feasible to treat every practice the same. Nor is it sensible to expect the same results and contributions from every practice. Some practices are well suited to attract new clients to the law firm. Some are well positioned to drive profitable revenues. Some are integral to maintaining a deep and lasting relationship with clients. Ideally, a firm should be able to define its expectations of each practice based on a portfolio analysis – and the practices should be able to pursue a valuable role within the firm in response to those expectations.

Portfolio management is a straightforward process in which management (or a strategic planning committee) assesses practices along two critical dimensions – the *attractiveness of the market* in which the practice group competes, and the *relative market position/strength* of the practice group. Each of these dimensions is discussed in more detail below.

Market attractiveness

The attractiveness of any given market is a function of a variety of factors – some purely objective, others more subjective. The key to using the portfolio analysis tool is to agree on a consistent set of "attractiveness factors" and each factor's relative importance.

Some examples of market attractiveness factors follow:

- *Competitive intensity* influences the attractiveness of a market. Highly competitive markets may not be as attractive as those with less competition. Note that competitive intensity reaches beyond direct competition among firms and is influenced by the buying power of clients, the threat of substitutes (think alternative legal service providers), and other factors;
- *Rate sensitivity* is an issue in many legal market segments. Markets or specialties that do or can bear premium billing are clearly more attractive than those with a high degree of rate sensitivity;
- *Market growth* is another obvious factor in rating the attractiveness of markets. Patent litigation was attractive throughout the 1990s and 2000s in large part because of the consistent growth in that market;
- *Market size* must also be considered. A large market is generally more attractive than a small one. A large, growing market is even better; and
- *The needs and demands of the firm's existing client base* is usually a factor. For instance, if virtually all of the firm's corporate clients need and use the firm's tax services, the tax market would be rated favorably on this particular factor.

Other factors might also be included in this analysis, such as historical or future profitability; regulatory and other external influences on the market; and the technology required (now and in the future) to compete effectively in the market.

Relative market position/strength

The other dimension to consider in a portfolio analysis is the relative market position of each practice group. The key word is *relative* – to key competitors and to the needs and expectations of the market.

Again, a variety of factors determine the relative market position of a practice. Some examples follow:

- The *relative quality of lawyers and/or work produced* is a key factor, but is often difficult to rate objectively. Third party ratings can serve as a proxy here (e.g., number of attorneys listed in *Leading Lawyers* or tier ranking in Chambers);
- *Practice profitability* (measured by contribution, realization, revenue per lawyer, net income per partner, or other means) can be an

indication of relative market strength. As noted above, profit potential can also serve well as a factor in determining market attractiveness;

- *Market reputation/perception* can be a strong indication of a practice's relative strength. Is the practice considered the leader, among the leaders, at parity with most firms, lagging other firms, etc?
- *Market share* – locally, regionally, or nationally – is another key measure of relative market strength. Unfortunately, law firms generally have to rely on the number of lawyers they have in a given area as a surrogate for market share. Nevertheless, share and share growth are good measures of relative market position.

Plotting the portfolio

Assessments of each practice group's relative market position and the attractiveness of the practices' respective markets can be viewed graphically by juxtaposing the two dimensions (market position and attractiveness) on a matrix. At a basic level, market attractiveness and relative market position ratings can be broken down to three "generic grades" – high, medium, and low.

The result is a three by three matrix like the one in Figure 1.

		MARKET ATTRACTIVENESS		
		High	Medium	Low
RELATIVE MARKET POSITION	High	Invest and Grow	Invest and Grow	Maintain/Pursue Premiums
	Medium	Invest and Grow	Maintain	Maintain or Divest
	Low	Improve to Survive	Improve or Divest	Exit

Figure 1: Plotting the portfolio.

A practice's position on the matrix provides direction on what strategies are appropriate for that practice group. The following points briefly describe these strategic implications:

- *Highly attractive, high relative position* – clearly the best of both worlds, this situation calls for aggressive investment and growth. In fact, others will envy this position and defensive strategies are also appropriate as the practice group expands on and consolidates its position.

- *Highly attractive, medium relative position* – this situation also warrants a growth-oriented strategy. However, an additional challenge is added in that the practice group also needs to find ways to improve on key factors that influence its relative market position.
- *Highly attractive, low relative position* – this situation poses a potential trap. The market is clearly attractive, but the firm's practice is a relatively weak player. In product markets, companies will try to double their market share in relatively short order or quit the market. Likewise, firms need to determine key milestones for practice improvement and move on if those milestones are not reached.
- *Moderately attractive, high relative position* – this situation warrants growth and investment. The practice's market position may also allow for relatively aggressive pricing and high profitability.
- *Moderately attractive, medium market position* – a solid practice in a mature market can and should be maintained and needs to be well managed. A well-executed maintenance strategy can yield satisfied clients and healthy profits for years.
- *Moderately attractive, low relative position* – if improvements cannot be made relatively quickly, a practice in this situation should be phased down.
- *Low attractiveness, high relative position* – while the market may not be attractive, the practice's strong position likely warrants a maintenance strategy. Furthermore, premium rates and premium clients should be pursued by a practice in this position.
- *Low attractiveness, medium relative position* – if the practice can be maintained profitably, do so. If not, a phased withdrawal is called for.
- *Low attractiveness, low relative position* – exit this market.

The matrix suggests relatively generic strategies. Naturally, the specific strategies a firm should pursue depend on many factors, some of which reach well beyond the scope of this analysis. Nevertheless, portfolio management is an extremely valuable tool in making resource allocation decisions among practices.

Reference

1. www.ark-group.com/product/balanced-scorecards-law-firm

Chapter 11:
Differentiation and innovation – enabled by culture

By David Urbanik, chief operating officer, Halloran Sage

Without an inspirational, dynamic, forward looking, strong managing partner, most law firms struggle to innovate. To the extent they do, it is often in the form of a random initiative developed by a particular individual or practice rarely duplicated elsewhere within the firm. Why is this so?

One reason is that law firms often look to strategic planning as the primary impetus for innovation. The planning cycle typically starts with a detailed SWOT (strengths, weaknesses, opportunities, threats) analysis from which a committee develops a set of detailed plans designed to move the firm forward. These plans are then presented and discussed at a partner retreat, generating energy, enthusiasm, and a commitment to action.

However, in most cases, the energy quickly dissipates as the pressure to produce billable hours and meet immediate client needs leads to a lack of follow through and a return to business as usual. There may be some incremental gain, but no game changers, and the strategic plan ends up as a pretty binder sitting on a shelf gathering dust.

This pattern demonstrates that the desire to innovate is not enough. Desire is something that people think and talk about. Firms must have more – the will to innovate. Will is about culture and sense of purpose. YOU MUST LIVE IT!

Developing the will to innovate in a law firm environment starts with recognizing that there is inherent incompatibility between many of the characteristics of successful innovation and several dominant personality traits associated with lawyers.

Successful innovation often requires:

- Dealing with the unknown;
- Taking leaps of faith;

- Collaboration and teamwork;
- Risk taking;
- Embracing the possibility of failure;
- Incremental steps taken over time; and
- Being open to critical review.

With this in mind, it is instructive to look at several personality traits highlighted in a study conducted by the consulting firm, Altman Weil, employing the Caliper Profile, a well-recognized test covering 22 robust traits. The study revealed that there are six traits for which the average score for lawyers is significantly different from the scores of the population in general.

The Caliper test grades each trait on a scale of 0 to 100 with 50 representing the median for all tested individuals. The traits that lawyers tend to score particularly high on are *Skepticism (90), Autonomy (89), Abstract reasoning (82),* and *Urgency (71).* At the same time, lawyers tend to score particularly low on *Resilience (30)* and *Sociability (7).*

- *Skepticism* refers to the inclination to doubt or question others' motives. Contrast a high score in this with the need to "take leaps of faith" often associated with successful innovation.
- *Autonomy* refers to the preference for independently determining work methods. Contrast a high score in this with characteristics associated with "collaboration and teamwork".
- *Abstract reasoning* refers to the ability to understand complex issues and integrate information. People scoring high like to deal with facts and logic. Contrast a high score in this with the need for "dealing with the unknown".
- *Urgency* refers to the tendency to take quick action in order to obtain immediate results. Contrast a high score in this with the need for "incremental steps taken over time".
- *Resilience* refers to the capacity to handle rejection and criticism. Contrast a low score in this with the need for "risk taking, embracing the possibility of failure, and being open to critical review".
- *Sociability* refers to the enjoyment of being around people and working with others. Contrast a low score in this with the need for "collaboration and teamwork".

When the above observations are combined with the fact that lawyers are trained to think and act based on precedent, are typically very busy, and take comfort in continuity and consistency, it is not at all surprising that promoting innovation is difficult in a law firm environment.

While the personality traits cited above represent the norm, there are clear exceptions. The inspirational, dynamic, forward looking, strong managing partner or the single lawyer implementing the random new approach likely does not fit the mold and probably has a much different Caliper profile. Nonetheless, most law firm managers who want to spur innovation are faced with a status quo dominated by these characteristics.

Halloran Sage clearly fit this mold when, in early 2017, it decided to step back and consider its future. Founded in 1935, it had spent the first 50 plus years of its existence becoming the premier boutique insurance defense firm in the State of Connecticut. Over the next 30 years it slowly diversified, evolving one lawyer at a time, to encompass a wide range of legal services for industries, institutions, business owners, individuals, and families. Over the years, the firm had enjoyed much success and stability and, as such, there was no clear mandate for change.

I had become familiar with a consulting firm, Fathom.net, during the previous year through involvement with a local non-profit agency. Fathom's main objective is to help organizations establish a clear vision for the future, help them realize their full potential, and put into action the goals and causes that will grow their businesses and positively influence the world around them. They do this by focusing on building and strengthening relationships and helping people better relate to each other and their work.

This prior experience led me to believe that interacting with Fathom could benefit the firm without knowing quite how. Over the next two years, with Fathom's assistance, the firm methodically went about answering the following six critical questions:

1. Who are we?
2. What future do we want?
3. Why do we do what we do?
4. How will we deliver value?
5. What unites us?
6. Where will we focus our energy?

In the process of doing so, it learned to think, feel, and act differently and, ultimately, developed tools to address and overcome organizational biases and inherent "lawyer" personality traits that were impediments to fostering a culture of innovation. A summary of that journey follows.

Question 1: Who are we?

We started the process with a survey of our key clients, team (owners and employees), and partners (vendors and referral sources.) The survey asked a series of open-ended questions designed to generate information concerning the following topics from all participants:

- Who are we for our world (clients, team, partners);
- What they see is possible for our future;
- What they believe we are doing or providing that is making the biggest difference; and
- How we could become more valuable for them.

Unlike client and employee surveys we had done in the past, asking for input by utilizing a rating scale for a broad range of defined characteristics, we found that the open-ended format produced a higher response rate and much more useful information.

In analyzing the survey results, many common themes emerged across all representative groups, which was both instructive and gratifying. However, even more valuable, were some notable differences between internal and external perspectives, as well as a few totally unexpected new insights about the firm. Collectively, the responses provided a solid foundation for discussing our desired future and what might need to change to create it.

Question 2: What future do we want?

Tackling this question began by gathering a small group of long-term partners involved in the management of the firm, along with several younger, recently elected partners, a total of nine people, for an intensive half-day workshop.

The session started with an assignment for each person to think of and record positive aspects of the firm, either in the form of something they personally had contributed to or had observed being demonstrated by others. As thoughts came to mind, recording them was restricted to a very specific format – a three-word phrase in the form of adjective–adjective–noun on a post-it note. Initially, almost all participants struggled with the assigned format as they discovered it forced them to think in a different manner. However, once they adjusted to it, ideas began flowing and approximately 140 phrases were generated relatively quickly and stuck up on a wall.

Three volunteers were then assigned to arrange the notes into clusters of related concepts and give each grouping a title. This resulted in eight groups – Finances, Management, Culture, Leadership, Community, Clients, Marketing, and Team/People. Next, individual members of the group were assigned one of the eight topics, given all the notes for that topic, told to incorporate every concept expressed in those notes into a piece of prose, and given about ten minutes to do it.

An unedited example of one of those ten-minute work products follows.

> CULTURE – *The culture at Halloran Sage reflects a forward-thinking mentality. A technologically savvy firm, Halloran Sage is populated by a diverse mix of attorneys from different backgrounds and age groups, working in cooperation in a team-oriented manner.*
>
> *The firm's calling card is a commitment to excellence – providing the highest level of legal work and advice to many types of clients. In a dynamic and collaborative fashion, the firm's many substantive practice groups adhere to the same general principles firm wide – the highest level of work product with a heightened sense of timely customer service and response.*
>
> *The firm's management is supportive on all levels, listening when necessary and providing guidance where warranted. A high premium is placed on mentoring to perpetuate the firm's continued evolution. The firm's coveted reputation in the legal community is derived from 80 years of fine legal work and will be carried forward to the challenges facing our clients in an ever-complicated future.*

This description provided a highly idealized picture of the firm, as did the other seven that were produced. The traits described certainly were not universally present throughout the firm. However, by virtue of the design of the exercise, there was evidence that each trait could be found, to a greater or lesser degree, somewhere at the firm. Basically, it presented what was possible if we focused on replicating the "best" of what already existed in smaller pockets throughout the entire firm.

Having generated a comprehensive idealized picture of the firm through the eight pieces of prose, the group then started an iterative process to distill and focus on the "most important" concepts. For example, relative to the culture description, the group by consensus extracted the phrases "team-oriented", "commitment to excellence", and "supportive at all levels". Once the most important phrases within each topic area were identified, the very most important of the important were called out through a process of elimination until there were just a few that could be captured in a single sentence which would describe a future we wanted to create for the firm. That sentence was:

> *A world of engaged, accountable people delivering excellence and fostering vibrant communities.*

This *vision* statement was then used as the focal point of a weekend off-site partner retreat with the following kick-off question being asked:

> *If the following was universally, demonstratively true across all offices and all practice groups – a world of engaged, accountable people delivering excellence and fostering vibrant communities – what would our world look like three years from now?*

After a brainstorming session, the following ideas emerged:

Bigger and better firm

- Substantial growth – establish a defined goal;
- Development of opportunities that we don't yet know exist;
- Profit rises – make more money with higher billable rate;
- Firm becomes more stable because it has fewer unknowns;
- Capacity to do work outside CT;
- Regional offices would be bigger and more central to the mission;
- More revenue from more clients, and more work to do;
- Enhanced and recognized brand;
- Reflects who we are/our future, not who we were in the past;
- Have more choices in who we hire, who we do business with;
- Finding rich sources of new business; and
- Seen as the "bet the company" firm.

More exciting, meaningful work

- Broader range of cases;
- Continually challenging ourselves;
- Different and better class of clients seeking H&S out; and
- Lobbying group is growing and more aligned with attorneys.

Taking more risk

- Spending time on things other than billable hours;
- Examining other ways to generate value;
- Letting go of legacy (commoditized) types of work; and
- Getting outside comfort zone and investing in new ways – outside commitments, mentoring, sacrificing some personal independence.

A thriving culture

- More personal and professional development – time to develop and grow;
- Committed to each other's success;
- Enjoying a higher quality of life;
- More people living up to the Vision;
- No closed doors in offices – "open feeling to encourage communication";
- More human interactions – face-to-face communication, less electronic;
- Increased accountability across the board;
- Sacrificing some personal independence – putting time into mentoring, outside commitments; and
- Sabbatical program.

More diverse and engaged workforce

- Adding more of what we aren't/don't have yet;
- A place that attracts top talent and retains it;

- More engaged females at all levels;
- Helping associates learn how to generate business;
- Developing future leaders – "Doers";
- Diversity of talent pipeline at all levels; and
- Succession planning.

Contributing to our communities

- Doing more politically, civically;
- Every equity partner would be on a board and would pave the way for/mentor others in the firm, too;
- Substantial involvement at law schools; and
- More pro bono work.

This picture of a potential future generated true excitement and a unanimous conclusion that the firm should invest time and money to take steps to create the foundation for pursuing such a future.

Question 3: Why do we do what we do?

This question is meant to get at the core being of an organization – its purpose. Purpose describes how our work will make life better for the people we serve, defining our work in terms of what we value and the effect we hope to have.

We explored this concept by asking about a dozen attorneys, representing a wide range of practices, to tell a story about when they felt extremely good about being an attorney and recorded their responses. Although each story was unique, in reviewing them a common pattern emerged. In its simplest form, the pattern was – client had a problem and in the process of addressing the problem an unexpected positive result or new opportunity emerged. Some examples were:

- A very contentious issue between two particularly acrimonious parties was resolved in such a way that the parties found common ground and a way to partner on future projects.
- Examining the problem at hand resulted in the identification of a previously unrecognized core problem with the client's business and the implementation of a plan to address the core issue.

- Delivering an unexpected financial windfall that truly changed an individual's life.
- Completing a transaction that opened an entirely new market for the client.

This led to the following proposition – would work be much more rewarding and enjoyable if, rather than letting such experiences be random occurrences, we took on every assignment with the mindset of consciously trying to create an unexpected positive result or new opportunity? Not surprisingly, this question was quickly answered in the affirmative.

After some discussion, this concept was boiled down to a few words which became our "why we exist" – our *purpose.*

Creating possibility through resolution.

The implication of this statement became to constantly look beyond accomplishing the specific task at hand and be ever mindful of doing more, opening doors, and creating new possibilities for the entire organization.

Question 4: How will we deliver value?

We used a structured discussion in a workshop facilitated by our consultant, Fathom, to find a bridge between our internally focused *vision* statement and externally focused *purpose.* That bridge would become our brand *promise* – what we are committed to providing the people we serve in every interaction, every day. It is intended to fulfill a core need and is something we can be counted on to deliver consistently.

By focusing on the concepts of "delivering excellence" and "fostering vibrant communities" found in our *vision* statement and "creating possibility" found in our *purpose*, our brand *promise* became:

The best path forward.

It is important to note that we are not using this phrase as a formal marketing tagline or slogan, although it may make its way, at times, into our communications. It is intended more as a guidepost for all our interactions with others, both internal and external.

Question 5: What unites us?

Given our *vision*, *purpose*, and brand *promise*, this question was aimed at defining the principles that would guide the behaviors of our organization and determine its priorities. In doing so, three parameters were set.

- Must be concise and easy to communicate;
- Should be limited in number; and
- Are non-negotiable – behavior inconsistent with the principles will not be tolerated.

Once again, we employed a facilitated, structured workshop in order to determine principles that met the defined parameters to arrive at an expression of our *values*:

- Clients, firm, self – in that order;
- Everyone needs to be essential;
- Excellence through collaboration and accountability; and
- Invest in knowing our communities.

Question 6: Where will we focus our energy?

In order to answer this question, we referred to our initial survey for grounding as to who we were and what we were perceived to be. We evaluated this against the concepts embodied in our *vision*, *purpose*, brand *promise* and *values* and identified broad areas of emphasis that we could use to generate specific action programs to move us towards our desired future. These became *mission* elements:

- Contribute to the vibrancy of our communities;
- Collaborate to define how we best serve each of our clients;
- Build an ownership culture;
- Invest in the development of our people; and
- Develop a firm-wide, structured approach to marketing and business development.

Pulling it all together

To recap, our *vision* statement defines the future we seek and informs our *purpose* and *values* which are brought to life through our *mission* and *promise*.

Vision:

A world of engaged, accountable people delivering excellence & fostering vibrant communities.

Purpose:

Creating possibility through resolution

Values:

Clients, firm, self – in that order

Everyone needs to be essential

Excellence through collaboration and accountability

Invest in knowing and supporting our communities

Mission:

Contribute to the vibrancy of our communities

Collaborate to define how we best serve each of our clients

Create and communicate a clear picture of success for the firm

Build an ownership culture

Invest in the development of our people

Develop a firm-wide, structured approach to marketing & business development

Promise:

The best path forward

Figure 1: Vision, Purpose, Values, Mission, and Promise.

The formal roll-out of these concepts began at an "all hands" firm meeting, which brought together every employee from our seven offices to one location for an afternoon. The meeting had assigned seating at round tables with a balanced mix of people from different offices, attorneys and staff, and men and women to leverage the value of different perspectives during discussions.

The meeting agenda focused on describing our journey to develop our *vision* and *purpose*, discussing the meaning and implications of the *vision* and *purpose*, presenting intended next steps to begin realizing the *vision*, and an interactive exercise with each table exploring the potential power of our *purpose* – "Creating possibility through resolution" – and then reporting out their results to the group.

This was an unprecedented and energizing event for the firm. It was quickly followed by a series of small group meetings of seven or eight people at a time in each office during which a "guidebook" was distributed and discussed. The guidebook conveys our *purpose*, *values*, *mission* and *promise*, as well as two additional fundamental elements – our *brand position* and *core story* – in an organized, integrated manner.

The *brand position* defines where we believe we fit in our marketplace of customers and competitors and carries the core information needed to create single-minded marketing communications. The *core story* is a narrative that captures the essence of our brand – our *promise*, key points of difference, *values*, core services – in language that appeals to both the intellectual and emotional needs of our client communities. These additional elements were developed by employing structured workshops facilitated by Fathom, similar to previously described exercises.

Implementing mission elements

We have developed a standard approach to moving the organization forward. It starts with identifying a specific issue/problem/opportunity related to a *mission* element. A team consisting of both staff and attorneys is then assembled to address the issue. Typically, teams consist of five to eight people and never more than a dozen. In some instances, teams are made up of volunteers based on interest in the issue. In others, team members are recruited by management based on known skills or abilities.

Once assembled, the team self-selects a leader, a recorder and any other roles deemed appropriate. The session begins by stating the issue/problem/opportunity being examined. The group then explores and records a picture of "success". Basically, the goal is to understand what positive change is possible before diving into a discussion of what is needed to get there or what barriers may be in the way.

The next step is to ask three questions:

1. What is working?
2. What is not working?
3. What is missing?

In most cases, there are multiple answers to each question. Recognizing that there are not unlimited resources of time or money, the group works towards developing a consensus as to which one, two, or, perhaps, three answers are most important to address. Once identified, an action plan is developed for addressing each chosen answer, responsibilities are assigned, and a timeframe for next steps is set.

The group then meets periodically to assess progress, adjust, and, if appropriate, move on to the next item to tackle until "success" is achieved.

Creating leaders

We encourage all employees to practice leadership, whether it be in the office, in their involvement in their community, or in their personal lives, and have developed a framework and tools to help. It starts with the core beliefs found in our "Declaration for Leaders at Halloran Sage":

- We cannot create outcomes.
- We can create conditions that support outcomes.
- Leaders create conditions through conscious actions.
- A conscious action is a choice made in a moment in time.

The Declaration goes further to define how we choose to act and the conditions we seek to create:

- Be unrelentingly kind.
- Demonstrate omnipresent respect.
- Be present with your purpose.
- Ask for help. Be ready to help.
- Cultivate connections.
- Take ownership of having others see where they can take ownership.
- Create and defend an environment that's open to everyone's ideas.
- Advocate for experimentation and opportunity.
- Challenge others with your admiration.
- Take down obstacles.
- Project an "open door" attitude.
- Contribute your approach to shaping ideas.
- Make it easy to share "success" and "failure".
- Encourage everyone (especially you).
- Surrender to possibility.
- Be accountable to yourself.
- See the whole picture.
- Talk about expectations.
- Make it safe to break new ground.
- Open your mind, again and again.
- Advocate for each other.
- Tell it like it is.

Each person at the firm has been challenged to review this list periodically and choose one or more of these aspects to consciously practice getting better at in their daily interactions. The point is to not look at the list and be content in the conclusion that "I do most of these things already" but rather to focus on actively mastering the ones that represent a challenge for the individual or to truly leverage an existing strength to benefit others and create value.

On a more formal basis, we have created a program through which individuals focus on a "breakthrough initiative". A breakthrough initiative is defined as being personally meaningful to the individual and in service to the future of the firm. Through this program, individuals are paired with a "buddy". Buddies act as mutual sounding boards, devil's advocates, and gentle nudges to stay on track.

The process begins with the individual identifying which of the above leadership traits they want to practice and where they want to apply it (or them.) The next step is to answer the following questions:

1. What is true now?
2. What is possible?
3. Why does it matter?

The answer to the first question grounds the person in reality. The second opens their minds to think boldly and creatively. The third provides meaning and motivation to act. Once these questions are answered, we employ the same three questions we use in our teams implementing *mission* elements with a bit more focus.

1. What is working? (What is contributing to that possible future right now?)
2. What is not working? (What current efforts will not lead to the desired future?)
3. What is missing? (What, if we had it, would make the biggest difference?)

We then add one more question. As a result of knowing these things, what action will I take?

This process is intended to be iterative. With each action taken, something is learned or changed and there is an opportunity to review the same questions again and identify the next action to be taken. Step by step, with the support of their buddy, the goal is to make what was initially identified as being possible into a reality.

Evidence of success

Two years after embarking on this journey, there clearly is a significant increase in communication and transparency at the firm. Our vision of fostering vibrant communities is being realized through organized efforts directed both internally and externally, creating greater visibility for the firm in our served communities.

Examples of service innovations include the development of a fixed fee General Counsel on-demand service, an insurance litigation guide, and a best practice approach to client onboarding.

A group of support staff have organized themselves as the Inclusive Innovators and have been responsible for implementing numerous initiatives to improve the efficiency of operations as well as build employee morale and team spirit.

We have totally redesigned our new employee onboarding process, starting from the initial job application to introduce what we stand for and actively involve new hires in building our desired culture. Our leadership program has led to successful initiatives such as tapping into a local improv comedy group to provide improv training to attorneys as part of their professional development or a staff manager overcoming shyness to reach out and develop a strong network of contacts throughout the firm and, in the process, become a confident public speaker and more effective leader.

The journey is far from finished. We would never have gotten as far as we have without the guiding hand, fresh perspective, and constant encouragement of our outside consultant. Moreover, maintaining momentum requires constant vigilance. At times, we must remind ourselves to use the tools we have developed. However, slowly but surely, we keep moving closer to realizing our *vision* and are a better firm for it.

www.ingramcontent.com/pod-product-compliance
Ingram Content Group UK Ltd.
Pitfield, Milton Keynes, MK11 3LW, UK
UKHW021834131026
9310IPUK00004B/74

9 781783 583782